microthrills

microthrills

true stories from a life of small highs

wendy spero

HUDSON
STREET
PRESS

HUDSON STREET PRESS
Published by Penguin Group
Penguin Group (USA) Inc., 375 Hudson Street, New York, New York 10014, U.S.A. • Penguin Group (Canada), 90 Eglinton Avenue East, Suite 700, Toronto, Ontario, Canada M4P 2Y3 (a division of Pearson Penguin Canada Inc.) • Penguin Books Ltd., 80 Strand, London WC2R 0RL, England • Penguin Ireland, 25 St. Stephen's Green, Dublin 2, Ireland (a division of Penguin Books Ltd.) • Penguin Group (Australia), 250 Camberwell Road, Camberwell, Victoria 3124, Australia (a division of Pearson Australia Group Pty. Ltd.) • Penguin Books India Pvt. Ltd., 11 Community Centre, Panchsheel Park, New Delhi – 110 017, India • Penguin Books (NZ), cnr Airborne and Rosedale Roads, Albany, Auckland 1310, New Zealand (a division of Pearson New Zealand Ltd.) • Penguin Books (South Africa) (Pty.) Ltd., 24 Sturdee Avenue, Rosebank, Johannesburg 2196, South Africa

Penguin Books Ltd., Registered Offices: 80 Strand, London WC2R 0RL, England

First published by Hudson Street Press, a member of Penguin Group (USA) Inc.

First Printing, August 2006
10 9 8 7 6 5 4 3 2 1

Credits: Ladybug art courtesy Age photo stock/ SuperStock. Page 9 diamond shapes art courtesy Wendy Spero. All photos courtesy Wendy Spero, except for pp. 101 and 201 courtesy AFP/Getty Images.

REGISTERED TRADEMARK—MARCA REGISTRADA
HUDSON
STREET
PRESS

LIBRARY OF CONGRESS CATALOGING-IN-PUBLICATION DATA

Spero, Wendy.
  Microthrills : true stories from a life of small highs / Wendy Spero.
    p. cm.
  ISBN 1-59463-019-14 (hardcover : alk. paper)
  1. Spero, Wendy. 2. Comedians—United States—Biography. 3. Actors—United States—Biography. I. Title.
  PN2287.S6642A3 2006
  792.702'8092—dc22

                                                                    2006008127

Printed in the United States of America
Set in Palatino

Some of the names and identifying characteristics of the people mentioned here have been changed. And because my mom seems increasingly alarmed by the notion of having her life revealed to the public, I thought I'd go ahead and make a special point that while the stories in this book are true, yes, technically, like in all nonfiction essay-type books, they are indeed created from subjective memories. My mother's recollections of certain incidents may differ. "Wendaay, you cannot say that the blue skirt we got from Loehmann's was polyester. It was not. It was a lovely marked down wool/cotton blend."

For Mom, Grandma, Grandpa, Gary, and Amos

contents

welcome to the microcosmos

So last Wednesday I sat in the corner of my blue sofa, intently squeezing the small, gel-filled rubber chicken attached to my keychain. I was pressing my thumb deeply into the chicken's breast region and then slowly stretching the pale skin, so I could see and feel the goo zooming around inside. I found this activity to be extremely enjoyable and yet, at the same time, maddening. I could not get into the mushiness *enough*. I longed for mushy closure.

I experience the same mix of joy and inner turmoil from those fruit-scented markers whose intense fruitiness is nearly infinite . . . it keeps going and going and going. Despite the escalating pleasantness of olfactory sensations, there is simply no fruity *climax*, goddammit. I just want to stick them SO far up my nose. But they only go mid-nostril. And that's not enough.

It's kind of like when I'm in a car during a slight drizzle. The precise choreography of the windshield wipers is mesmerizing, but I am slightly irked by the thin wet arc left behind by the first stroke. I get this peculiar feeling inside and think, "Get rid of that line." Sure enough, they go the other way and efficiently erase that line. But then another line is formed, and I think, "Get rid of *that* line." It's back and forth and back and forth—the ultimate emotional rollercoaster. And then there's that little triangle of mist in the center that never gets touched at all. EVER.

Cute babies provoke a similar feeling of endlessness. They are cute, cute, and *continue* being cute. I love them *too* much. I want to consume them. My cousin's baby is the cutest baby ever to exist. He is super-fat with a dour expression, like a mini-emperor. His cheeks are so heavy that he could use a cheek bra. His thigh is a juicy calzone. People are always saying, "Oh look at that child. He's soo cute. I could just *eat him up!*" But I mean it. I wanna slab on some savory marinara sauce and be done with it.

Anyway, after forty-five minutes of sitting on the couch, absorbed in poking and pressing the rubber chicken, my boyfriend, Amos, casually glanced over in my direction from his desk chair in the adjoining room. Just as he rolled his eyes at my latest infatuation, the trinket literally burst open, squirting my face with lime green toxins, temporarily burning my skin and probably clogging my pores. But it was so darn worth it. Not only was the relief extraordinary, but the moment was shared with someone else.

I mean, if a rubber chicken squirts you in the face and no one shares it with you, did it really happen? Not completely. It's sort of like bungee jumping—I'd imagine the event really isn't over until you get home and start making some phone calls.

See, I want to live on the edge, to the fullest, but I'm not the bungee jumping kind. I'm petite and easily trampled in crowds. I won't put my head underwater. I've never learned how to ride a bike. I'm probably allergic to bees. There are few traditional outlets for thrill-seekers like me, so I find excitement where it feels more manageable—in a world filled instead with bursting rubber chickens, smelly markers, and edible babies. It is a world containing everything that feels compelling or out of the ordinary, but not too dangerous or threatening. It is my small, safe, fun compromise between adventure and banality. And like the world of bungee jumpers, it is usually better once it's shared.

The characteristics of my world became clearer to me a few months ago, after some friends and I rented a French documentary called *Microcosmos.* The film opens with dramatic violin music and wide-angle shots of a vast, empty field. Slowly, the camera goes deeper and deeper into the grass, taking you into a very specific, self-contained insect universe. I dislike actual insects with a fiery passion, but somehow seeing them magnified on screen is massively entertaining.

In one of my favorite parts, five or six furry, plump, purple-and-green striped caterpillars march with utter purpose in a strict line along a small mound of dust. Two strays successfully weave themselves into the formation. Soon, more and more join the group. Intense thumping sounds accompany the strutting and you wonder, "Holy shit. Where are they headed? What's so important?" Then the camera pulls out: they are going in a circle.

Later, two hesitant virginal slugs enact the *most* graphic sex scene. With operatic tunes swelling in the background, they become entwined in one jiggly, oily mass. During the drawn-out foreplay, the awkwardness among my friends was palpable. Everyone fell silent and avoided eye contact. We were vaguely, disturbingly turned on.

Toward the end of the film, pouring rain thrashes down onto the field. The caterpillars are forced to abort their circle and anxiously wiggle for cover. The slug sex comes to a screeching halt. Eventually, though, the weather clears and the quirky rituals begin again.

As the credits rolled, everyone agreed that the movie was

good, but I alone maintained that it was hands down *the best*. I loved that it celebrated a strange kind of smallness. And I related to the concept of a microcosmos, a small world brimming with tiny thrills, tucked away within a large, scary, confusing macrocosmos; a small world always at the mercy of inevitable outside forces.

A life spent on such a small scale can be frustrating, but mostly intensely pleasurable—in its own bursting-rubber-chicken kind of way.

And it's so much more satisfying when it's shared.

shoulder padded
muuutual masturbation

With antiaging cream glistening from her pores and the thin, red belt of her plaid robe dragging a foot behind, my elfin mother would often burst into my room at night just as I was attempting to unroll a Trojan condom onto the absurdly oversized schlong of my relatively petite high school boyfriend. She'd put her hand in front of her eyes and meander across the room saying, "Don't mind meee . . . continueeew . . . continueeew . . . I'm just coming through for a moooment, guys . . . to get some thermal leggings . . . don't mind meee. I'm almost gone . . . almost gone . . . and GONE!" By the time we'd hear the last and thunderous "GONE!" she'd be back at the threshold, reaching to close the door and offering a mini goodbye wave of encouragement.

My mother wasn't trying to interrupt. She was a single parent who, for the past seventeen years, had selflessly given me the master bedroom of our small, one-bedroom, Upper East Side apartment. She slept on a pull-out couch in the living room, and all of her nightgowns, skirts, blazers, blouses, brooches, clip-on earrings, and pumps were kept near my bed, in and on top of a long oak dresser. In the connected master bathroom was the deep sink that she used for the constant hand-washing of underwire bras and nude control-top pantyhose. So she'd often need to come into my bedroom during the evening to retrieve key belongings or tend to the thick Ivory bouillabaisse of soaking undergarments.

When walking past us, she'd be sure to tiptoe. (Because it would, of course, be the *footstep noise* that would ruin the sexual momentum.) And most of the time, even if my mother flipped the switch when entering, the overhead light would not go on because she has never grasped the concept of changing bulbs. (Only two or three small, decorative lamps around the apartment would be working at one time.) Regardless, as soon as the door cracked open, my poor young gentleman suitor would scramble for the starchy sheets, turn pale, and mumble, "Hi Mrs. Spero, nice to see you, uh . . . thanks for having me over again . . . is that a new robe?" But I'd smile and appreciate the sublime bizarreness of the moment. Not unlike the way I appreciate a boiled beet. It's sort of gross, but also sort of sweet.

I was used to the parent/sex overlap. My mother decided to expand her social work practice and become a licensed sex therapist three months after my eleventh birthday—at the exact *millisecond* I began considering, for the first time ever, what it would be like to roll around half-naked on the grass with Gary Carter, the burly old catcher for the New York Mets. His trunk-like arms simply oooozed eroticism, and when I watched games at Shea Stadium on TV with my grandfather, I'd notice Gary cradling the ball and think, *He'd surely cup a plump boob in the same delicate way.* Mom once returned from her evening sex-therapy course and caught me sitting an inch from the television screen enraptured by a steamy sex scene in *Falcon Crest*, fantasizing about the curly haired Mets catcher tenderly caressing my jaw before trailing his stubby fingers down my torso. Attaché case still in hand, she made sure to set me straight.

"Wendaay, sex is NOT like what you see on the television. Do you hear me, dear? Real lovemaking involves active communication. Active, *active* communication. A full exchange of information and needs. And a lot of hard work and compromise. Sex is not naturally perfect, like it is in those *highly* dramatized scenes." I was super bummed to hear this. But I nodded and promised to always convey needs, although I had no idea what a "need" might be.

Within weeks of starting her sex-therapy training, my mother had morphed into a younger, less wrinkly Dr. Ruth. She had always been short (around four foot eight) with pixieish, dyed blond hair, but she started to talk ever more slooowly, her chin pointing downward and her eyes blinking carefully and thoughtfully as if perpetually analyzing the quality of your sex life. Her nine inches of shoulder pads solidified the persona. Not only would she attach the thick oval pillows both under and above her bra straps with velcro, but she'd wear an airy blouse with built-in pads, a lightweight cardigan with built-in pads, a quilted jacket with built-in pads, and finally a long wool coat with, of course, built-in pads. This gave her small daintiness a vague football quarterback quality. Two tall, soft towers stood on either side of her neck and sometimes they ascended so high that gravity would take its toll and I'd have to shuffle them back into place like a steep stack of cards.

Since my mother had now technically become an expert, overflowing with detailed, juicy knowledge, I began asking her to weigh in on my sex-frequency estimates: After exiting the double doors of our high-rise apartment building I'd ask, "How often do you think the doorman has sex?" After leaving a family friend's Passover seder in Long Island I'd ask, "How often do you think that bearded man who hid the matzoh has sex?" After seeing an ambulance go by I'd ask, "How often do you think the

EMT people have sex?" Her answer to these questions was always the same. "Probably twice a week, dear." Twice a week didn't mean anything to me at the time, but I made sure to memorize the statistic, stashing it away for future use.

Because my mother purchased an overabundance of literature for her sex therapy research, as puberty kicked in and my hormonal urges increased, so did the number of graphic sexual diagrams in my immediate vicinity. On the dining room table, among the electric bills and tax forms and Bloomingdale's receipts was a book titled *PE: The Ups and Downs of Premature Ejaculation*. It contained detailed drawings of every possible sexual position, some of which were so complicated-looking that they would seem to require years of targeted muscle development. After examining each of the contorted images, my friends and I would write the names of our teachers next to the naked participants. Not in pen, though, because as soon as we got bored imagining Mr. O'Reilly, our hefty math teacher, straddling Ms. Schwartz, our disheveled principal, upside down on the dangerously narrow wooden swing, we'd need to contrive an even more profound faculty concoction.

In ninth grade, I started dating the well-endowed gentleman suitor, who later became the High School Boyfriend, after he sent me a tiny, crumpled note in Biology that said, "Je tame." He was blond and just slightly taller than me—maybe five foot two—and looked a little like Calvin from *Calvin and Hobbes*, but with a wider nose. My mother thought he was just precious. She made it a top priority to nurture our sexual curiosities, and to ensure that her daughter was getting high-quality action in the sack. If he was over on a Saturday afternoon, she'd offer to go to Barnes and Noble or the Guggenheim Museum for a few hours to get out of our way. "Wendaay, this way you can explore one another's bodies without worrying about me coming in at all."

I'd be like, "Maaa, please, it's fine. Don't be ridiculous." It seemed wrong to kick my mother out of her own house so I could practice giving mediocre hand jobs. But it was nice to know that she was ridiculously flexible in case of a horny emergency down the line.

Keep in mind that in New York City there are no "make out points" at the top of hills and barely any high school kids know how to drive or have access to a car. Sometimes, we got so desperate for privacy that we'd go to second base in dark movie theaters or in certain extra-wide dressing rooms at the Gap. Usually, though, we just opted to risk it and mess around in my trundle bed, knowing that at any moment my mother might waltz in to return a geometric-shaped brooch to her jewelry box or to stir her soapy broth of delicate fabrics.

One Sunday during my junior year, while my mother and I were washing dishes in the kitchen, I complained about our predicament: "It's just frustrating because his house would be a perfect place to hook up in, I mean, he doesn't share part of his room. But his parents are more conservative than you, and they won't let us be alone in the house. It's so ridiculous too, because we're not even having sex or anything yet . . ."

My mother looked more concerned than she did the time I threw up an intact carrot at age five.

"EXCUSE ME?"

"What? Not every parent is as liberal as you about this stuff, Mom."

"YOU'RE NOT HAVING *INTERCOURSE* YET?"

"Oh. Well . . . no . . ."

"Why not?"

"I . . . I dunno. Well, he's too big, actually."

"Too big? Are you properly luuuubricated?"

"Yes."

"Well, do you precede insertion with forms of muuutual masturbation?"

"Eew. It's called a hand job Mom, and yes."

"Noooo, dear, there's something better than that."

And then she reached into a pile of Julia Child cookbooks and pulled out her prized sex torah, a clump of crinkled, yellowed pages that had been separated from its cover and spine, and that had clearly been written by some erotic guru long ago.

Let's just say it was the greatest, most informative sex manual EVER, which ultimately . . . made me very popular.

It's probably not a coincidence that when we first started hooking up, my college (and current) boyfriend, Amos, complained that I was overly analytical in the bedroom, often ruining the moment. ("Could you move your hand about two inches to the right? I'd also like you to stroke my thigh if/when you get a chance, in a lighter, but not too light, manner. Thanks. You got it. No, now that's too light. That tickles in an annoying way. There. Sustain that. Proceed.") And that when I graduated from college and lived back at home for a year, Amos and I kept our sex life to the confines of his bedroom in Brooklyn. Occasionally, though, he would sleep over in my old room when we needed to stay in the city. After getting ready for bed, Mom would poke her head into the doorway and yell, "Wendaay! How do you expect to seduce poor Amos tonight if you are wearing that smelly green acne mask? It'll ruin the moment, dear. Wash off the mask for heaven's sake." Amos would smile and nod, and I'd drag myself to the bathroom to make myself more presentable to my man. And more important, to my critical sex therapist.

On those nights, Amos and I chose to keep things PG—we knew we had a private apartment to go back to the next day.

Plus, it was more fun to just lie quietly and wait for my mother to tiptoe through. "Don't mind meee . . . continueeew . . . continueeew . . . don't mean to interrupt anything, guys . . . just coming in for a second . . . really . . . I need to do a quick hosiery rinse . . . if left in too long elastic can get worn down . . . anyway . . . don't mind me . . . almost gone . . . almost gone . . . and GONE!"

einstein, the filmmaker

My grandfather resembled a tanner, bushier version of Albert Einstein. The huge mound of thick white hair pouring out of the back and sides of his head perfectly matched the abnormally large white mustache that took over a quarter of his face and conveniently soaked up any sauce or liquid he consumed.

In order to maintain his look, every summer he and my grandmother, a busty woman with permed gray hair and a cane, would rent a condo in Fort Lauderdale where he'd put on a tight black string bikini, fluff up his mustache, lather his equally hairy body in scented oils, and lie out in a plastic beach chair while holding a silver platter to reflect the rays toward his face. During the weeklong visit I made every year, my grandfather and I would take strolls on the beach and he'd look so striking that we'd get stopped by numerous people eager to take his photograph. After enthusiastically offering at least five different practiced poses (smiling with arms at hips, serious with arms crossed, profile with arms at sides, etc.), he'd seize the opportunity to publicize his self-published book, *Diamonds, Love, and Compatibility*, which analyzed the relationship between the shape of an engagement ring and the potential for disaster in a marriage. (He wrote the book after retiring from a lucrative career in gemology.) He'd tell the innocent beachgoers about his press clippings from the *National Enquirer* and his appearances on network news shows in Japan (to which he'd made numerous trips for business purposes I've never understood) to perform what he called the Diamond Shape Game. If they were a couple, he'd take out a Diamond Game cheat sheet, which he kept secure behind one of the elastic bands of his bikini, sit them down in the sand, ask each of them their diamond shape preferences, and declare whether or not they should bother staying together.

There were six diamond choices (round, marquise, oval, heart, square, and pear—see figure 1), and as soon as you'd number your preferences from one to six, he'd gasp, fiddle with the unruly hairs on his face and let out a hearty "Woooowww. Yikes. Interesting stuff." Then he'd shake his head in wonderment and mutter things like, "Well, Marsha. It's Marsha, right? Marsha, Marsha. Boy oh boy. There's certainly a lot going on with you, dear. You are a real swinger. Meaning you like to have fun. But you sometimes like to take it easy. At certain times you're a real homebody—aren't you, Marsha?"

Marsha would raise her eyebrows and say something along the lines of "Yeah, I mean, I don't like to be at home generally but there have been times . . . yeah, totally. Oh my god, that's *crazy* that you can tell that."

My grandfather championed his diamond theories anywhere

FIGURE 1

| Round | Pear | Marquise | Square/Emerald | Oval | Heart |

and to anyone who was polite enough to sit through them. For my tenth birthday my grandparents took me to a semi-fancy Italian restaurant on the Upper West Side, and as soon as we were seated, he started chatting up a woman with a protruding jaw and tousled dirty blond hair sitting alone nearby. She told us that she was a singer, and my grandparents thought that was "just darling!" and went on and on about how brave she was to have made such a risky, artistic career choice. They had such a terrific rapport that she decided to join our corner table. When the moment was right, my grandfather slipped out his Diamond Game cheat sheet from his pant pocket, analyzed her diamond choices, and told her to get into therapy ASAP because she'd have problems committing.

Then he reached into my grandmother's handbag and handed his new friend a free, signed copy of his book. (My grandmother always carried extra copies, in case of emergency.)

The woman seemed charmed by his unique charisma and politely thanked him for the advice and gift. When the cake arrived, she happily belted out "Happy Birthday" along with my grandparents. After we hugged her good-bye and parted ways, our effeminate waiter came running after us screaming, "What was she like?"

"Who?" my grandmother asked, picking a piece of almond out of her teeth.

"Carly Simon!"

"You know her?"

"She's only the most important singer of all time!"

"She's a famous singer? How lovely for her! We were concerned; I mean it's hard to make it as a singer in this town. She did hit the notes quite well in the birthday song. Good for her. She'll need that career stability when her romance falls apart."

I only truly appreciated this encounter after I saw *Working Girl* with Melanie Griffith and got all inspired during Carly Simon's rendition of "Let the River Run."

What kills me, though, is that I cannot find this episode of our lives in my grandfather's comprehensive "Wendy Archive" home video collection. In addition to religiously espousing his radical views on gemology, my grandfather made it his life's work to capture seemingly every second of my childhood on tape, which he then logged into a comprehensive library. Birthdays were the least of it. My grandparents lived only ten blocks from my mother's apartment, and I spent every Sunday for the first nineteen years of my life in their small, elaborately decorated penthouse apartment as the subject of a surreal reality show. Their one and only grandchild, I'd walk through the door greeted by applause. "Our queen has arrived!" they'd holler. And the distant little red light of my grandfather's gargantuan 1980s video camera would start to blink.

The thing is, my father was their only child. He died unexpectedly at the age of forty because of a hospital mishap during a relatively minor operation. I was ten months old at the time. So it's no wonder they were obsessed with preserving every moment of my life.

Their penthouse apartment made for a slightly inconvenient film set. My grandmother had been a professional interior designer, and had arranged the living room to look like a roped-off museum exhibit featuring the extravagant home décor of eighteenth-century nobility. Chairs upholstered in rust-colored wool and rickety wooden tables and benches surrounded a large fireplace. In the center was a tall, thin antique pedestal that proudly displayed my grandfather's book. My grandmother had also spent a considerable amount of time adorning every inch of the apartment with tiny memorabilia from the many trips she and my grandfather had taken over the past fifty years— countless miniature ceramic dolls from Italy, coasters from South America, hand-painted spoons from Holland. Once, when one of my weekly performances (a particularly rousing rendition of Cyndi Lauper's "Girls Just Want to Have Fun" involving a lot of sweeping hand gestures) got out of control, I knocked an Italian doll off a side-table, shattering it to bits. Of course, my grandparents didn't blame me—they appreciated the importance of my artistic development. But afterward, my grandmother carefully secured the tchotchkes to all vertical and horizontal surfaces with that blue sticky gunk you use for posters in college.

Occasionally, I'd agree to share the spotlight. My best friend Maya would come with me to their house for the afternoon, and we'd change into our matching purple stirrup pants and rhinestone-covered sweatshirts to create music videos for our professional rap routines. (Maya and I made a point of dressing alike most of the time, even though she was significantly taller than me and had thick curly black hair, which, for an unfortunate period of time, was overly feathered because of a careless hairdresser in the neighborhood.) Our biggest hit, "Like-a

Reeelly Cool," was shot on the terrace because the lyrics demanded an outdoor backdrop. We would take turns, one of us singing a verse while the other made guttural noises as hip accompaniment. ("Ooo, ooo, uh-uh-uh, ooo, ooo . . . It's like-a reeelly cool and like-a reeelly neat that my house is located ON my street, oh yeah. It's like-a reeelly cool and like-a reeelly neat that the songs I'm singing RHYME to the beat, oh yeah.")

These video shoots were often frustrating, however, because we obviously had no editing capabilities and relied solely on my grandfather to turn the camera on and off at a precise moment. We'd hit the final "Oh yeah!" and then stare blankly ahead in silence, waiting for him to move the lens away or press stop. One of us would murmur, "Psst! Now! Cut!" but he'd stand there chuckling as we'd get increasingly bossy, stomp our feet, and beg to take it once more from the top.

When I wasn't performing, my grandfather enjoyed mumbling into the camera's mini-microphone. If I ever walked away for a bathroom break, he would aim the lens at a random crack on the wall and talk about the water leakage from the neighbor's bathtub. Or if I was sitting on the bed, exhausted, showing my Garbage Pail Kids cards to my grandmother, he'd just stand like a crazed stalker in the corner of the room focusing in on my chin and muttering, "It's a nice day out but they said it might rain later . . . I hope it doesn't rain since the Mets are supposed to play this afternoon . . . Wendy has a good chin. Look at that chin there. Now from this angle. Wendy, darling, pick up your chin up a bit. Give us a wave over here. Chins are an important part of the face, actually, though they go unnoticed . . . Is that thunder?" He was barely audible over the strange buzzing sounds of the zoom feature.

Sometimes he'd get emotional. "Wendy," he'd sigh, "you look so cute sitting there with Grandma . . . being so perfect and wonderful. One day you'll be watching this when you're all grown up. I might not be around then, but you'll have this recording of me talking."

At the time, I thought, *Whatever*.

His video monologues became more frequent during a two-year stretch in grammar school when I came down with an unexplained long-term dose of laryngitis. Although I sounded like Demi Moore and received nonstop compliments on my raspiness, it took every ounce of energy to utter a single syllable. This condition was particularly frustrating during slumber parties when my friends would scream over one another to share thoughts on the charm of Garfield versus Odie or whether either of them out-cuted Ziggy. In order to contribute to the discussion, I'd have to raise my hand like an overzealous pupil. Eventually one of the more observant girls would see my eagerly erect arm and say, "GUYS! Quiet down. Wendy has something to say. Shhhh. Wendy?" Then I'd whisper my opinion, which was no longer pertinent because they had already moved on to sexier topics, like Ouija boards.

Because the laryngitis period seriously hampered my ability to project, during visits to my grandparents' apartment, I was forced to spend many silent hours sucking ice pops and playing tic-tac-toe. In order to keep the ongoing video documentary as dynamic as possible, my grandfather would report the latest political news while filming the inking of every *X* and *O*. "No performances again today," he'd mumble. "Wendy's voice still just gets lower. But in contrast, there's been a dramatic rise in Reagan's deficit spending . . ."

The camera made the most sense at school functions. And thankfully, he filmed my award-winning fourth grade performance in *You're a Good Man, Charlie Brown*, which took place during the laryngitis years. My teacher/producer had to write me a silent part. Because Charlie Brown mentions his crush on a little red-headed girl, the teacher had me wear an Orphan Annie wig and said I could be A Little Red-headed Girl who would sit mutely on a bench in one of Charlie Brown's scenes. While all the other kids frantically marked up their pages to memorize multiple lines, I had half of a stage direction highlighted in yellow (*"Charlie Brown stands at stage left."*).

My grammar school was a happy, nurturing, private institution that ran from kindergarten through eighth grade, with twenty-four kids per year (split into two classes of twelve). It was a small, red-brick building next to a skyscraper and across from a crowded park with a swing set, where we'd sometimes have recess. The classrooms were spotless and overly modern— ever since the school had been donated a huge sum of money from a wealthy alum, pristine-looking desks and top-of-the-line Dustbusters had been installed in every room.

Because the faculty was big on family-teacher interaction, every spring the school celebrated Grandparents' Day, when grandparents were invited to an assembly in their honor, and asked to sit in on a full day of classes. This was my favorite event of the school year because my grandfather, with his clunky camera permanently glued to his face, was revered like some form of video god. Most people had only seen cameras like his on TV. The curious kids would come running up to examine the massive contraption; the annoying ones would fight for the camera's attention; the adults would blush, giggle, and wave. It was especially amusing to watch the stricter teachers get increasingly flustered by the camera's presence during their overly rehearsed lessons. Not only were they being judged by involved grandparents, but their teaching methods were also being permanently documented so they could be heavily mocked by me and my stoner friends twenty years later.

One year the local Channel 2 news team did a racy special on the elderly's involvement in youthful activities and decided to cover our Grandparents' Day merriment. When the reporters caught sight of my grandfather's Einstein magnificence, they rushed toward us for an interview. My grandfather was thrilled by the notion of filming the reporters *while* they were filming him. It became a showdown.

"Uh, sir, please put down your camera so we can film you for the news."

"If you're filming me, I'm filming you."

"We can't see your face when you talk, sir, please."

My grandfather reluctantly took the lens off his eye but held the machine tight to his chest. He held me close under his other arm. When they asked him to describe our relationship, he took a deep breath and uttered, "She is my *immortality*."

His quote, along with an image of me looking excruciatingly uncomfortable, appeared on the local ten o'clock news. Although my grandfather was unable to record the scene from his perspective, he managed to set the VCR that night and include the segment in the ever-growing video diary of our lives.

It would be pertinent to add here that this was not the first time I had heard him mention the immortality thing. When I was in preschool, I'd be happily shoveling in the sandbox and he'd lean in and whisper, "Remember, you are my *immortality*, Wendy."

It was a bit much to absorb at age four.

I'd shyly reply, "Thanks?"

After my father died, my grandparents understandably just shifted all of their focus and attention and love and purpose in life onto me. They would sometimes call me by his name. By mistake.

"Gary, go get the ricotta cheese from the kitchen."

"Sure." *Oy.*

In fact, my grandmother had a habit of nearly fainting at the

mention of my father's name. Toward the end of my uber-Reform bat mitzvah service, for which I only had to recite phonetic Hebrew, the rabbi announced, "Will everyone in mourning, please rise." And—*twelve years* after my father's death—my grandparents *rose*. But, swept up in the emotion of it all, my grandmother couldn't deal, so, as she stood up, she fainted and fell to the ground. Only moments after the congregation let out a collective gasp, two ambulance men in white coats came running up the side aisle and took her away. I was in a panic on the pulpit, but because I'd heard from my mother that she had fainted before, I knew she'd be okay. And at the reception she was her normal, jolly, outgoing self—with an ice-pack attached to her head. Luckily, this event was caught on tape, too. It starts out with this boring religious service—*Baruch atah*, shalom—and all of a sudden, grandma's DOWN. It never gets old.

Whenever the subject of Gary was brought up, or whenever I did something small and cute that reminded them of him, my grandparents wouldn't say, "Oh, your father liked cucumbers too . . ." Instead it was, "Let's take out the album and talk about how you must carry on his legacy. And weep." Watching my grandparents choke up during a perfectly pleasant game of hangman made me writhe in discomfort, so, with them at least, I avoided the topic of my father at all costs.

My mother took an entirely different approach to Gary. She had two eight-by-ten pictures of him on an antique wooden table in the living room, but mentioned him rarely, never forcing the subject on me. I think she took the "when Wendy's ready to ask, she'll ask" approach. Or maybe it was too painful for her to discuss. Or maybe she feared she'd open herself up to me too much and that that would somehow make her a bad parent. (My mother has always been so selfless that she never wants to burden me with any of her personal problems. She can talk to me for hours about how to find my G-spot, but she had surgery on her foot seven years ago and didn't tell me until *last October*.) If anything, my father's role in our lives was de-emphasized because we both called him by his proper name. Never "Father" or "Dad." Just Gary. I knew that a man named Gary had technically been involved in my existence, but as far as I was concerned, I'd been born from one parent. And I was so attached to my mother that I never felt a void in the family unit. The mere thought of having a second parent to worship was overwhelming.

While my mother was not opposed to my grandfather's excessive filming in and of itself, she found the underlying fixation with me as a surrogate child a little unsettling. She loved my grandparents like they were her own parents, and was very appreciative of their financial and emotional support, but at times they seemed to overstep boundaries. They'd come over to babysit at least once a week and end up enrolling me in dance lessons, rearranging our furniture and closets, and inserting doilies under plates and saucepans in the cupboard.

My mother also frowned upon the excessive amounts of spoiling that often accompanied the video shoots. Things got particularly tense on my ninth birthday when my grandparents had us over for dinner and presented me with a huge, gift-wrapped robot, mainly so they could film me opening it. Because my grandmother also liked to exercise her creativity through cooking, that night she served chicken cutlets floating in Minute Maid orange juice. My mother refused to eat the concoction, so when it was time to open the massive present, she was already cranky from low blood sugar. And nothing makes a cranky person more cranky than being filmed from every angle and being told repeatedly to put on a happy face for the camera.

"Come on, let's see one smile for the viewer. Just one. There you go. I see the beginning of one. Look right into the lens. *Right* in the center . . ."

"Saul, enough."

I bit my pinky hangnail and leaned on the side of my ankle, hesitant to rip off the shiny red wrapping, knowing that the present underneath would probably be too extravagant and that Mom would not be pleased. (My mother objected to frivolous, overly advertised games, like Twister or Hungry Hungry Hippos or Lite-Brite or the Snoopy Snow-cone Machine. Instead, I owned many generic stuffed animals and we played a lot of Sorry and Uno. These were not particularly educational activities—I mean, Sorry was just like Candy Land except that you were supposed to yelp "SORR-Y!" every time you sent your opponent home—but to her they seemed better somehow for my moral fiber.) Yet I forged ahead with suppressed excitement and, after tearing away the paper, an awe-inspiring four-foot-tall cyborg stood before us in all its round-eyed, silver-plated, triangular-headed, rectangular-torsoed glory. According to the box, the robot could move around on wheels via remote control and serve drinks on a special tray (not included). I anxiously looked back at my mother for her approval. But she had that strained "they did it again" look on her face. She could not contain her anger and, after closing her eyes for a good five seconds, blurted, "I can't believe you bought her a robot. It is totally indulgent. If you wanted to get her a computer, fine. This is just . . . I . . . I just . . . *fine*."

"But she gets whatever her heart desires," said my grandmother, adjusting her bra strap. "And she has mentioned wanting a robot for months."

"No, she doesn't. That is not how it works, Judith. I . . . *Fine*. Wendy, get your coat, it's getting late."

It's so wild to be able to watch this kind of childhood family dynamic unfold on a twenty-inch television set. My grandfather caught every single expression up close. My eyes are shifting back and forth, and I'm biting my lower lip—I clearly cannot fully enjoy the gift knowing that my mother disapproves, but am trying to filter out the adult power struggle and appreciate its brilliance.

For the next two weeks, my poor mother arrived home from work exhausted to the dull sounds of the slow, cheaply made Robot Man 5000 circling around her like a shark. Because I discovered that I could project words from the robot's mouth by talking into a small microphone on the remote, the robot nagged her constantly: "Please accept me into the family. I'm a new friend of Wendy's. I'm better than an educational computer. I can serve you drinks as soon as Wendy is allowed to buy my special tray!"

Like all of our electronic devices, the robot broke after two weeks but remained in the house for decades. It sat quietly by my bookcase, so every time a new friend came over, they'd scream, "YOU HAVE A ROBOT!?" and I'd have to break it to them slowly. "Yeah, it's supposed to serve drinks. We never bought the tray. The batteries ran out. Then something else went wrong. I don't know why we still have it. I'm so sorry."

As soon as I entered high school, I went from being an annoying ham who got a kick out of my grandfather's camera to an obnoxious teen who refused to be filmed. My mother and I would walk into the penthouse, and I'd flip my hair back and forth, roll my eyes, and make a snarky comment about how lame it was that he couldn't put the contraption down for even two minutes.

My grandfather would reply, "Wendy, don't be a crab. This is all for you and your memories. So tell the camera about high school. What's your favorite subject?"

"Ugh. I dunno. Who cares?" I'd storm into the bathroom to reapply my brown lipstick and talk on their cordless phone with the High School Boyfriend, bemoaning the existence of all adults.

When I started college and visited the penthouse during summers and on breaks, my grandfather would sometimes feel too weak from his blood pressure medication to carry the heavy camera around the apartment. (He was too emotionally attached to his original model to ever upgrade to a newer, lighter one.) He'd instead have me set up a tripod and would watch from the bed as I'd talk to the lens about dorm life or read from my Womyn's Studies papers. And twice he let me film *him* as he reminisced about his fame from the Diamond Shape Game.

Before he died a couple of years later, my grandfather asked that he be buried with a copy of *Diamonds, Love, and Compatibility* and a pile of pictures and video tapes of me through the years, which probably included the long lost Carly Simon episode. It was touching. But there is something highly disturbing about the fact that buried in a graveyard somewhere are wacky eighties images of me in fluorescent yellow parachute pants, attempting to do the moonwalk.

Last month my grandmother turned ninety-eight years old. She is honestly the spunkiest, happiest, most thriving person on earth. When my grandfather died she moved to one of those old-age villages in Fort Lauderdale and eventually started poetry and painting classes at the recreation center. Soon after, she became a local celebrity. I'd call my grandmother to tell her I had a good stand-up set, and she'd reply that her abstract painting was just named best piece of the year by the artwork committee at the local clubhouse. And that she'd just been interviewed by numerous medical journals about the issues facing the geriatric community. And that one of her witty poems about the city bus was just accepted to be published in the *New York Times*.

Doctors cannot wrap their heads around her. Every time my grandmother sees new specialists, their eyes widen with bewilderment as she lays the groundwork: "Before we start, you need to know you can't pull any condescending old lady stuff with me. I read the newspaper front to back every day. I'm exceptionally 'with it.' It's almost scary." She'll complain to me that the nurses aren't attractive enough. "I just can't bear to look at this one woman's nose. It's impossible to get good help that has any sense of style."

She also has an entourage of male suitors who pay her visits and send her flowers. She'll tell me, "I can't be bothered with any of them. All these old guys are so homely and have no sense of humor. It's almost insulting that they think they'd have a chance with me, ya know?"

If only they could see the tape I recently found in a tucked away video storage bin.

Turns out my grandfather was quite the filmmaker long before I ever came into the picture. When I first watched this batch of converted black-and-white Super 8 film footage, I went through a range of emotions. "Oh my goodness, my grandmother looks so young and stunning . . . I guess she's trying on some new lingerie . . . no, she's doing a STRIP TEASE. OKAY, WHY do I have a Paris Hilton video of my grandmother doing an erotic dance for my grandfather? And she's flashing! Actually, she has a nice ass . . ."

There is obviously something disconcerting about owning porn of your grandparents. But how many people can say that when they listen to their grandmother adjusting her hearing aid on the phone, they can't help but picture her licking her lips and caressing her perky cleavage at age twenty-five?

Luckily, I also found footage of them having romantic picnics with potato salad, and cheering my father on as he adjusted his robe at his college graduation. I even found a clip of my grandfather frantically typing the first draft of his manuscript in his den.

They were stars in their own movie, instead of extras in mine.

live-in sidekicks

Beedee and Gaga, my imaginary friends, were fraternal twins. Beedee was a thin, dainty redhead with good posture who liked to wear long, pale yellow turtlenecks. She resembled a No. 2 pencil. Gaga, on the other hand, was short and pudgy with curly black hair. His nasal passages were permanently clogged, so his voice sounded muffled. He often dressed in denim from top to bottom. I met them both one sunny day in the Central Park Zoo, by a duck pond, and suggested they come back to our apartment and live inside the dark wood cabinet in the living room, where Mom kept the liquor. They immediately got into the Scotch and started a drunken ruckus.

I specifically liked the fact that they were siblings, while I was an only child. I never felt like a third wheel around them; in fact, I relished my role as mediator of their rivalries. It was gratifying to break up their fights about the most random little shit, like who got to enter an elevator first. Although I recognized that they sometimes enjoyed one another's company, especially when reminiscing about their family vacations, I often thought, *I should really thank my lucky stars I don't have to deal with that sort of thing.*

Not only did sibling relations strike me as competitive, but I couldn't imagine really going the distance during a temper tantrum with another kid in the household potentially judging me. Once, in first grade, I asked my friend Jessica, who had a slightly younger sister, "But, so what happens with your sister if you start crying and freak out? You know, I mean, if you do that sort of thing."

"What do you mean?" She answered, tightening her pony-tail. "If I start crying my sister just sits quietly until it's her turn. Sometimes she freaks out about things too, and I'll just watch on the side."

I replayed this comment in my head for years. Her sister really observed while she lost all control? Did Jessica not feel remotely censored by the presence of a witness? I still think that if anyone besides my mother ever saw me throwing forks across the room, tears streaming down my face and screaming, "Nooooo! I hate you! I won't eat bow ties! *They get overcooked on the flaps!*" I would have been outed among my friends as a serious psycho.

Once my imagination could no longer sustain the existence of Beedee and Gaga, and having friends that were imaginary became very passé, I started fantasizing about having a real, sibling-esque, live-in sidekick. One that would always be available to keep me company and one that wouldn't be smart enough to judge my hysterical behavior. Adopting a mentally challenged human seemed unlikely, so one Friday evening, when I was six, I sat my mother down on the tan, suede love seat next to her sofa bed and officially addressed the topic of pets. She was cautiously open to the idea.

Dogs were out of the question, obviously, not only because they would require walking, but because both of us were (and still are) deathly afraid of them. No matter how innocent-looking or domesticated, there was never a 100 percent guarantee that dogs wouldn't freak out and attack and give us rabies. Whenever we passed someone on the street walking a dog, we'd instinctually link arms and shuffle to the edge of the sidewalk. Luckily, we didn't know too many people with dogs, but whenever I had a playdate with a kid who owned one, the parents were explicitly told by my mother that it would have to be locked in an extra bedroom or in the closet for the duration of my visit. (Dogs have always reminded me of those kids in elementary school who had chocolate ice cream smeared on their faces after lunch and who were a little bit too gung ho about dodgeball. They were the same kids who were sooo happy to see me, even though they barely knew me, and who seemed to lack the ability to take a deep breath and quietly study the subtleties of life.)

Mom majorly disapproved of cats as well because they would require a smelly litter box. That was fine by me because I had recently been traumatized by two twin felines at my friend Hannah's house on Roosevelt Island, a New York City neighborhood that was most easily accessed via an aerial tram.

I had been hesitant to go to Hannah's house for a playdate because it meant committing to a sleepover with her during the week. (There was no way to have a simple after-school get-together with Hannah because no sane parent or babysitter would travel in the evening to pick you up from so far away.) A school-night sleepover was normally the best thing that could happen to a first grader, but I'd heard that Hannah's family was Christian Scientist and wouldn't allow medicine in their home. My friend Emily had experienced extreme sinus pressure during her overnight visit to the house, and Hannah's mother didn't have any form of decongestant. Or even Tylenol. Instead, she ordered Hannah's younger sister, who had a severe lisp, to pray for Emily's health by her bedside.

I eventually got sick of turning down Hannah's invitations, though, and I had my mom make arrangements for a night on Roosevelt Island. I was thankfully pain-free for the entire time but instead was severely tormented by her two cats. Emily had not warned me about this aspect of the Hannah-sleepover experience. She had probably been too distracted by the praying, lispy younger sister to notice.

Hannah had long limbs and beady green eyes, and looked a little like a cat herself. She spent a majority of our time together holding the cats, sometimes both at once, cooing, "Oh my God, HOW cute are my babies? How cute are they? Don't you just love them? Look at them!" She spoke in a perpetual baby voice. (Baby talk should only be permitted if you are alone with a human baby or cuddling in bed with a significant other.)

I don't usually notice the appearance of cats because they all look the same to me, but believe me when I tell you that Hannah's cats were downright homely. Apparently, they had some rare disease that made them want to eat themselves, so chunks of their fur and flesh were missing. Their gray eyes were also puffy and glazed over. They obviously had some form of pink eye and were deprived of proper eyedrops because their owners were Christian Scientists.

Like all cats, Hannah's cats crawled all over me. Sensing my aversion, Hannah scolded them. "Guys, Guys! Leave Wendy alone. Now's not a good time." But she could not enforce the order and reverted right back to "Aw, they love you. Look at that. They never respond to strangers like that. Oh my God, how can you not just love them?"

Later that night, after Hannah's mother had turned out the lights, the cats crept from Hannah's bed onto my adjacent sleeping bag and situated themselves across my stomach. Since I don't know how to lift cats, I tried nudging them repeatedly, and spent at least thirty minutes pleading, "Shoo, shoo. Go away, kitties. GO!" But they just glared back at me with conjunctivitis-covered corneas. The next day, I went to school severely sleep deprived and stinking of gross, ugly cat, and performed less than favorably on an important math quiz.

Mom and I briefly discussed the possibility of fish, but there was no point in pretending that they wouldn't die within days and ultimately be a waste of everyone's time. Plus, if my pet was really going to be a surrogate sibling who'd make me feel less lonely, it would have to be one that could chill out on land. We considered gerbils and guinea pigs but were told that they made too much noise at night with their treadmill-type wheels. Then I remembered being most impressed with a talking parrot on *Sesame Street*. A pet who could actually converse in *English* seemed ideal. Mom and I agreed that a bird would be a nice compromise between unsocial fish and overeager mammal.

At the local pet store the next day, I peered through the glass at hundreds of swooping birds, trying to make eye contact with one of them in order to find some existential connection. At the top right corner stood a quiet green parakeet that seemed introspective, philanthropic, and down-to-earth. I had it ushered into a box for ringing up.

When we got home, we set up the small, triangular metal cage on top of the piano in the living room, and named it (we forgot to inquire about gender) Green Parakeet. I spent the rest of the weekend with my nose an inch away from the bars of its cage, repeating my first and last name in hopes that it would learn to address me in a humorously formal manner: "You're a good egg, Wendy Spero. You, Wendy Spero, make a fine owner." But it just chirped, pecked the bars, and cocked its head to the side all snotty-like.

After a couple of days, my mother and I found it easier and

more time effective to refer to Green Parakeet as G. P. and after a couple of weeks, we started referring to the bird as "that bird." If we ever addressed the bird directly, we'd coldly say, "Bird, *please*. Quiet down, bird."

One day the bird got out in the apartment when Aida, our caring and attentive housekeeper from Ecuador, was replacing the newspaper at the bottom of its cage. (Both my mother and I were scared to clean the cage ourselves, lest the bird get angry, puncture our skin, and give us an avian virus.) It headed straight for the large window in our living room, which was closed, smacked into the pane, and landed on a moist mound of soil in a small planter. (Our windows were often rather smoggy so you'd think even a dumb bird would detect *something*, but no.) The bird survived, but must have suffered some form of brain damage, because within hours it became angry and loud and even more uninterested in me. Its chirping during the day on weekends was so distracting that Mom had to put a towel over its cage so it would think it was night and fall asleep.

My only positive memory of the bird was the time it acted as a justice of the peace at my friend Soomee's guinea pig's wedding ceremony. My mother's colleague, who lived in a building across the street from us, had adopted Soomee from Korea when she was three years old, and we'd been friends ever since. We had frequent playdates, usually including my friend Maya. Soomee and Maya were also only children with pets, and the three of us often talked of planning an activity with our respective animal sidekicks. One Saturday afternoon, we decided that Maya's obese male guinea pig, Scurry, should tie the knot with Soomee's small female guinea pig, Nobie. The marriage was in every way arranged because the pigs could not have been more incompatible. Nobie was shy and sweet and followed orders: *Stop. Go. Eat.* Scurry, on the other hand, was belligerent and seemed slightly uncomfortable in his own skin. It probably didn't help that Maya enjoyed wrapping him up in a beach towel and swinging him around and around for hours in a counterclockwise motion.

We arranged to carry our pets to Soomee's house the following weekend, and on the morning of the big day, while Soomee's mother was busy on a long-distance call in the kitchen, we decorated Soomee's bedroom with confetti and pig treats, placed my bird in its cage on a shoebox/altar, played the invigorating theme song from *Free to Be You and Me*, and let the pigs loose down the "aisle" we'd created by pushing her toys and stuffed animals to the side. The pigs immediately started licking the pathway because I had spread a thin layer of cream cheese all over the hardwood floor. (I'd figured it would make the surroundings as shiny as ever for this special occasion *and* be tasty for the bride and groom.) The bird paid no attention to any of us and furiously ripped apart newspaper bits, but we mimicked vows and shoved the couple into a nearby closet for a quick honeymoon. When we opened the door, there was pee and throw-up covering pairs of sneakers, loafers, and Mary Janes. I hadn't known the couple was lactose intolerant. But overall it was a decent time, and I'm the first to admit it wouldn't have been the same without the presence of my lame-o bird.

My growing lack of interest in the self-involved bird meant that I still felt a need for a live-in buddy. A pet I could really befriend. Like—a turtle. My favorite book as a kid was *Eloise*, which was about a little girl who grew up in the Plaza Hotel in New York City, and she had a devoted turtle that she kept on a leash. So I requested a devoted turtle that I could keep on a leash.

My mother made a couple of phone calls and discovered that

little snapping turtles were diseased and dangerous, but that larger, palm-sized turtles were completely benign. Through a random connection of a family friend, we somehow obtained one of these things and placed it (again, we never inquired about gender) next to two supposedly "stimulating" shiny flat rocks in a thick glass tank the size of a small microwave. It sat on a shelf in my room between a stack of Uno cards and the Sorry box.

My mother and I came up with the name Slowpoke. Ironically, when I tried to attach a thick string around its mid-region to act as a leash, Slowpoke became the fastest reptile of all time. It bolted under my bed and we had to retrieve it with a broom.

The next day, when I got a good look at Slowpoke's face, it stared back at me with evil, yellow eyes. It looked a little like a female librarian who was tired of all the cataloging and desperately in need of a moisturizing facial. Even when I touched its shell while it was safely in the tank, Slowpoke rejected my friendly advances by pulling its arms and legs inward. After two or three days, the name Slowpoke got replaced with "that turtle."

Because its tank was so heavy, my mother asked Aida, who was very strong, if she wouldn't mind cleaning it out in the bathtub. But she usually only came once a week, and sometimes didn't have time for the tank, and periodically went on vacation. After a few months, the poor turtle's home became a smelly, toxic, mossy, oily, algae-filled disaster area. Since my mother and I often forgot we owned a turtle, Aida also took on the responsibility of feeding it. We quickly ran out of the pet store stuff, so Aida began sprinkling cereal near the turtle's mouth. Sometimes I'd casually look over and see a lot of swollen Cheerios floating in the water and wonder if the thing was getting its proper nutrients.

Once I woke up in the middle of the night and saw the turtle standing on its hind legs, trying to coordinate a *Shawshank Redemption*esque escape. I cried out to my mother for help, but the turtle fell back into the toxic water when it heard my voice. I considered letting the animal go in Central Park near other turtles, but Mom said it would die instantly because it wouldn't know how to socialize properly. It was too depressing for words: the turtle hated its life, had no way out, and couldn't even commit suicide. I had a recurring nightmare that it would eventually climb over the walls of its tank, and, seeking revenge, attack me with soggy bits of wheat.

Visitors would come to our house, see the turtle, and be like, "What? *Eew*. What is that? You have a turtle? I didn't know that. How long have you had a turtle?"

My mother and I would simultaneously lower our heads and mutter, "Yeah, I don't want to talk about it."

Mom had heard that these turtles could live up to a hundred years, so I often imagined myself as an eighty-year-old woman, dragging the thing to a retirement home in Boca Raton. It was clearly going to outlive us all, despite its sketchy meal plan.

Thankfully, the turtle saga ended well. Two years after I graduated from college (so that's, what, almost twenty years later?), my mother was talking to a colleague who randomly mentioned that he loved turtles, and he happily adopted it. So Slowpoke's probably doing really well now, and I like to think it has forgotten about the horrible years it spent as an outcast in the Spero household. But I still feel enormous remorse about what went down.

When I was about eight years old, once it finally became abundantly clear that live animals would never provide the kind of unconditional companionship I was looking for, I seriously zoned in on inanimate objects. I did not respond to dolls, however, which struck me as too gimmicky. I remember gazing into the window of a toy store near our apartment and despising, on sight, one doll called Oopsie Daisy, "There goes li'l baby!" It was a fairly realistic-looking, pigtailed, plastic toddler that appeared to be falling down a steep set of stairs. Its arms and legs were spread in every direction, bracing for impact. On another shelf was Baby Shivers, a soft premature infant in a frilly blue onesie that vibrated like it had pneumonia. It also peed if you squeezed its foot. I had no sympathy for the odious thing, despite its obvious suffering.

Stuffed animals, however, suddenly seemed deeply soulful. They had always appeared cute, but I realized that unlike pets and high-maintenance dolls that were programmed to urinate, they would not actively require feeding and upkeep. And they wouldn't try to escape. They were 100 percent pure unadulterated everlasting adoration. They were exactly what I'd been looking for.

Around this time, I read a book about a small teddy bear named Corduroy who anxiously sat on a white shelf in a big department store, hoping to be purchased by a kid who would love him and give his life meaning. For years, I had had a hunch that stuffed animals were really alive underneath all that fake fur, but this book sort of sealed the deal for me.

Soon, every time I'd make eye contact with a stuffed animal, I was convinced they were trying to communicate with me, like a psychic who believes he alone can hear dead people gabbing. Whenever I'd pass a toy store, stuffed animals would chaotically scream out to me. They were thanking me for believing in them and, coincidentally, begging me to take them on as unconditionally loving sidekicks.

Unfortunately, whenever I was lucky enough to enter a toy store, Mom would only let me pick one animal. I'd lift the Chosen One from the pile and desperately try to avoid looking at the others, whose eyes bore into me with anger and jealousy. I so wanted to whisper, "I'll return for the rest of you. Just give me some time . . . ," but refrained because that would have gotten their hopes up.

There was no *one* stuffed animal that ultimately filled that sidekick role. It was my diverse collection of thirty that eventually did the trick. (Among them were Theodore, a large elephant hand puppet; a stiff five-foot-tall Pink Panther given to me by my grandparents; and a nameless, soft, pilly lizard purchased at the museum of natural history gift shop.) However, I was not prepared for the inevitable anxieties that came along with the newfound intensity of these relationships. Sometimes I was asked, "Which is your favorite stuffed animal?"— in my room, *in front of all of them*. I felt like they were all staring at me, waiting for my reaction. Like there was a drumroll and one would be declared a winner. I resented being put in that position and would sternly declare, "I don't play favorites." And I really didn't. But that also meant that at night, in between nightmares about being attacked by my turtle, I'd wake up in sweats after envisioning a fire running through the house, and the horror of having to choose which ones to save.

My mother put a cap on my collection the moment I met the stuffed animal of my dreams. When I was about twelve, my mother and I passed a toy stand at JFK airport on our way to visit my grandparents in Florida. I tried to look away, but the passionate, googly eyes of a floppy-eared dog met mine, and said, "I'm the one. Really. I'll be the most important one from this day forward." I thought he was probably being overly dramatic—I mean, he was the only one left of his kind, and was shelved next to newer-looking, fluffier stuffed animals, so he'd probably been rejected for months. But a small voice inside my head (different from the husky voice I was channeling from the dog's mouth) said that he really was special. That he wasn't just cute. That he could change the entire course of my life.

I listened to my intuition and stated calmly and carefully, "Mom. Listen. We need to go back to get a floppy dog. I know I've said this before, but this time is different." But once Mom was in airport mode, no rational argument about the fate of a desperate stuffed animal would sway her. The aircraft ended up being delayed, and we waited at the gate for two hours while I screamed in vain. "We can still go back! There's time!" I am not exaggerating when I say that every few weeks since then, I have thought about that dog and how we could have gone back. There was time.

I also still feel remorse about inflicting extreme violence on one of my favorite teddy bears, about ten years ago. When the High School Boyfriend broke up with me during our sophomore year of college, the only thing I could think to do was to take a three-hour bus ride home to my mom's house to rip the arms and legs off of the life-size brown bear he'd bought me at FAO Schwarz, for our first anniversary, when we were fifteen. Yarny bits sprang from its sockets. But because I could never ever throw away a living, feeling stuffed animal, my mother and I wrapped its body in Saran wrap and placed it on the top shelf of my bedroom closet, where it couldn't remind me of the fuckface who had broken my heart.

The High School Boyfriend and I got back together that summer, but a year later, when he broke up with me for the second and last time, I headed straight home and pulled the teddy bear off the shelf by a dangling plastic strip, forced it to the ground, and tore off its head. My mother came rushing in and took the torso to the incinerator—the seams were coming apart and we were about to have a serious mess on our hands—but I insisted that we keep the head. *Its eyes were still looking up at me.* From then on, a huge teddy bear head remained by the dark turtle tank. Whenever new friends from college would visit me in the city they'd become overwhelmed with confusion. "Wait, you have a gross turtle? Is that thing alive? Hey, does that robot work? Why do you have a huge teddy bear head on the shelf? Who *are* you?"

When Maya and I used to fantasize about being grown-ups who lived in our own apartments with our own sets of silver-ware, we'd talk about how utterly cool it would be to own as many stuffed animals as we wanted. And to never have to ask permission to buy more. And to not have to keep them sequestered in one bedroom. "We'll decorate our kitchens, hallways, dining room tables, and coffee tables with stuffed animals!" we'd sing. I'm still very much in touch with Maya, and when she visited me and Amos last week in Los Angeles (Amos and I have temporarily moved from Brooklyn to West Hollywood for work stuff), the first thing out of my mouth when she walked into my home was, "See? I kept my side of the bargain."

Maya was sufficiently impressed by the abundance of stuffed animals arranged strategically throughout our apartment. In front of the faux fireplace, along the longest wall of the living room is Carol, a four-foot-tall, beady-eyed penguin with a woolen scarf tightly wound, babushka-like, around her head. Looney, a slightly crazed-looking ape, lives on the mantle.

Through the wonders of stick-on Velcro, he is holding Eugene, a thin, fragile monkey, who, in turn, is holding Mr. Miagi, a small orangutan resembling the wise man from *The Karate Kid*.

On opposite sides of our big, blue couch sit two blissfully ignorant-looking snowmen, Steve and Dave, who wear red fleece jackets and pom-pom hats. Their arms are spread out as if they are in the midst of an elaborate tap dance. They have "jazz hands" inside their black gloves. Bob, a third snowman from the same manufacturer, stands in the corner of the bathroom because his light blue fleece matches the flowery tiles. He appears slightly retarded or something because his face is off kilter and an overeager dog once ate part of his left eye off.

In the center of it all is my favorite (these days I don't mind playing favorites): Joyce, a male rabbit gardener, whom I actively think about and miss throughout the day. He was given to me in college as a birthday present, and from the moment we met I just knew he was born male, named Joyce, and had a fluid gender identity. It is Joyce's ensemble that says "gardening." He came wearing a flowery blouse, flowery shoes, a blue-jean jumpsuit, and a matching jean visor. He sits quietly at one end of the long, low coffee table in our living room, on a little wooden chair meant for a child that I purchased at a flea market. Positioned by his right paw is a thick brass belt buckle that says "JOYCE" in a graffiti-type font. (It was a necessary forty dollar purchase from a vintage store in Hollywood.) By his left paw is a paper cup connected to novelty plastic spilled ice cream. He is a rabbit taking a break from gardening, lounging at the table with his nameplate, and spilling his dessert. It's a breathtaking diorama.

After Maya surveyed the stuffed scenery, she looked at Amos sympathetically and asked, "So, Amos, how do you feel about all these creatures?" Amos rolled his eyes, and explained that

sometimes it's pretty weird to yawn and stretch to the side in the morning and find himself staring into the eyes of a miniature frog reading a miniature book on a miniature red-painted rocking chair that has been positioned in the corner of our bedroom. "I do sometimes wonder just how far this is all going to go," he admitted, removing a finger puppet from under his shoe.

But then I told her that the first time I really thought Amos might be a keeper was during our senior year of college when he engaged Joyce in an in-depth conversation about gardening in the oppressive summer heat.

As our relationship has progressed, Amos has become more than merely tolerant of the growing number of stuffed animals in my/our life. He seems equally interested in their well-being. It was he who suggested I take Carol, the penguin, to the big Hollywood premiere of the documentary *March of the Penguins* last month. As my college friend Rachel and I waited in line by the red carpet (live penguins from SeaWorld made an appearance), people kept pointing at me and asking, "*Oh my.* Where did you get the penguin?"

"I brought it from home." I responded proudly, adjusting the knot of Carol's miniature scarf.

When I got back to the house that night, I found Amos holding Eugene (the fragile monkey) in his lap while watching ESPN and chugging beers.

And just the other night Amos and I were having a candlelit romantic dinner when he randomly asked, "So how do you think Otto is adapting to the California weather?" (Otto is a stuffed ostrich who has five wool scarves permanently attached up and down his long furry neck.)

"He's been staying inside on the chair by the window in the bedroom," I replied. "Near the breeze. He might be hot, but it's better than those seriously humid days of summer in New York. Plus, whatever, Otto is the type to adjust wherever he goes. He has a solid sense of self and is unfazed by lifestyle changes."

"Yeah, totally."

This kind of elaborate make-believe talk is not some sick fetishy form of foreplay. Quite the contrary—our hour-long parental discussion about Otto's quirky love of winter accessories not surprisingly killed the mood.

And yet, one of the highlights of our relationship occurred a few months ago when we found Guisseppi, a thin, malleable giraffe, mysteriously keeled over in the kitchen next to an empty glass beer bottle. The next day I decided to encourage the debauchery and rearranged some objects in the house after Amos left for work. He returned home that evening to find Walter, a striped donkey-like creature, smoking from a small glass bong. Snowman Dave was on the dining room table, attempting to snort crushed Ritalin. Snowman Steve and Carol, the penguin, were engaged in a "sixty-nine."

When I got home late that evening, I found the stuffed animals lined up neatly on the couch. Dave was listening to classical music from an iPod. Steve and Carol were watching the Discovery Channel. Walter, the donkey-like dude, had made his way through half of *War and Peace*. Bob, the vaguely retarded snowman with a wandering eye, was eagerly reading a placemat.

Amos and Otto were sound asleep, spooning in bed.

e.t. and ocd

I blame it all on Steven Spielberg's *E.T. the Extra-Terrestrial.*

As I followed Maya and her father down the dark exit ramp of the small Upper East Side movie theater, I knew I would never be the same. The film had punctured a hole in my innocent core, and with every step, all the remaining sanity in my seven-year-old body leaked onto the popcorn-covered carpet. Not only was I still alarmed by the image of E.T., all white and sunken and connected to monitors with suction cups, but, more important, I was deeply traumatized by the fact that for the majority of the movie, Elliot, the kid, was *the only person on earth who knew the alien existed.* Yes, he chose to keep the alien a secret and yes, E.T. happened to be harmless and very nice. Irrelevant. Forced to analyze E.T.'s existence by himself, on some level, Elliot must have worried that no one would believe him if he tried to explain it.

So I started to worry, too—not that I'd see an actual alien, but that an alien might appear in my room one night, hang with me for a little while, maybe play a couple rounds of Uno, and then disappear before anyone else could see it. The sighting/interaction would be too much to process alone and worse, what if no one believed me? Before long, my biggest fear in life became the possibility that I'd befriend an alien who'd refuse to meet anyone.

To be fair, *E.T.* might have just unleashed some issues that had been percolating since I first began watching an abundance of *Sesame Street* at age three. Fundamentally, I liked this show. I'm all for harmonious interactions between furry creatures and humans. But as wholesome as *Sesame Street* was, there was one deeply upsetting character dynamic: During the years I watched the series, Snuffleupagus was not yet an acknowledged member of the *Sesame Street* clan. He only appeared in scenes with Big Bird, and would accidentally wander off RIGHT before another character came along. When Big Bird raved about his very real furry best friend to Mr. Hooper, Maria, Oscar, and the others, they'd be like, "Sure, Big Bird. Whatever. You have a 'best friend.' Dream on." Big Bird tried to be a good sport about it, but he'd still plead, "No, you guys, really, I have a *best friend*, he was here just a second ago!" I was shocked and outraged by their lack of faith in Big Bird. The misunderstanding was gut-wrenching. I wanted to dive into the screen and shake them ferociously and make them believe.

After Maya and her dad walked me home from the movie theater that night, I begged my mom to let me sleep on the tan love seat near her sofa bed. That way, if I saw an alien, friendly or unfriendly, she'd probably see it too. But unfortunately, Mom had a new boyfriend over. She had always casually dated, but this guy was one of the few significant long-term suitors. I'll call him Ron because I've never really liked that name (I apologize if your name is Ron). Ron was a financial analyst who had an oblong head and a nasty space between his two front teeth. He and my mother had only been going out a few months, so the answer to my request to sleep on the love seat was an emphatic "no."

"But I'm really scared this time," I begged. "All those other times were *nothing* compared to this." Mom might have felt badly, but she held firm, and I was forced to curl up at the edge of my bed in a fetal position and yell for her reassurance through the wall from my room.

"MOOOOOM!! IF AN ALIEN DROPS IN AND TALKS TO ME BUT GOES AWAY WHEN YOU COME IN, YOU PROMISE TO BELIEVE ME THAT IT WAS HERE. *RIGHT?*"

"I'D BELIEVE YOU *THOUGHT* YOU SAW AN ALIEN, DEAR!"

"YOU NEED TO SAY YOU'D BELIEVE THAT THERE REALLY WAS AN ALIEN!"

"BUT THERE IS NO SUCH THING AS ALIENS, SWEETHEART. I'D BELIEVE YOU *THOUGHT* YOU SAW ONE."

Ron probably cursed the day he got involved with a single parent because we must have gone back and forth like that for forty minutes and for an hour every night thereafter for the next six months.

Now that I think about it, the whole E.T./Snuffleupagus thing was sending a severely harmful message to children. I mean, what about kids who had actually seen or experienced something really bad? In fact, I just learned that this was why the producers eventually integrated Snuffleupagus into all *Sesame Street* social gatherings. All children must be told they'll be believed! (Mark my words: the first thing I'll do when my baby comes out of the womb is look it straight in the eye and say, "I will totally believe you if you ever see or befriend an alien.")

Shortly after seeing *E.T.*, I instituted a formal under-the-bed check for potential aliens. I figured that if I could spot one before it jumped out and surprised me, I'd have more time to alert my mother so she could see it for herself—more time before it rushed off to its spaceship. But checking under the bed was not a "quick glance and then you're done" type of thing. Because I

had a trundle bed, a bed with another bed on wheels folded underneath, I'd have to flip myself upside down, craning my neck
inward so that I could carefully look between all the metal bolts
and bars. A small alien could easily perch itself on one of the
ledges.

Once the area under the bed was fully surveyed, I'd lift my
aching neck and body upright to continue scanning the remain-
der of the room like a responsible lifeguard overseeing a large
pool. The thoroughness felt satisfying. But after a few seconds,
it would occur to me that in the time it took me to lift my head,
an alien could have scurried under the bed. I'd be upside down
again as quickly as possible to take another look. And then
again. And again. I'd bob up and down like this for hours, gripping my pink sheets for assistance. Eventually, at around midnight, having given myself a headache, I'd pass out from
exhaustion.

After a few weeks, I finally became convinced that aliens
were not coming to befriend me. But I continued to check under
the bed to fulfill a lingering urge. I didn't enjoy the checking,
but even after the twentieth bob, I'd come up, feel dizzy, pause,
and think, "Just once more. I'll feel fully content after *one more
look*." During sleepovers, I'd try to mask the ritual by throwing
my pillow on the floor. "It just keeps falling! UGH. Guess I gotta
bend down and get it again . . ."

Checking under the bed was soon accompanied by an increasing number of compulsions involving smelling, pressing,
and hugging.

The first began with one of my square, smelly Hello Kitty
erasers. One day, while watching *227*, I became fixated on its intense strawberry aroma. I remember sniffing it for hours on end,
bringing it slowly toward my mouth, and being truly torn.
"Must taste good . . . so smelly . . . No, it's an eraser." Finally, I

just went for it and took a huge bite, which caused my entire body to convulse in disgust. A couple of minutes later, I found myself gnawing on it again.

Before long, I couldn't leave the shower without smelling the caps of my shampoo bottles for a good ten seconds each.

And I couldn't pass by my closet door without pressing my pinky into a specific crack in the white paint near the knob.

And I couldn't get into bed at night without hugging each and every one of my stuffed animals until I could feel their innermost stuffing crushed between my chest and hands.

I once overheard my grandmother speaking on the phone. "It's so cute that Wendy feels she must hug her animals before bed." I remember thinking: *This is not cute. This is pure madness.* She didn't understand. I wasn't hugging my animals because I loved them so much (even though I did love them dearly). I was hugging them because the thought of not giving in to my impulses to crush their innermost stuffing on a nightly basis was just . . . psychologically painful. Resisting these urges would have been like suppressing the desire to lock the final piece of a huge, complicated jigsaw puzzle into place. Or holding back a massive sneeze. Just not possible.

Unlike checking under the bed, I never attempted to hide these additional longings and tics because that would have required energy I simply didn't have. I'm not sure why, but my mother never seemed to notice. Peers did. Every now and then a classmate would plead, "Wendy, stop smelling my cheek."

Then, the summer after *E.T.,* when I was eight years old, I was overwhelmed by an inexplicable need to cover my neck. Mom had enrolled me in a small day camp in Riverdale, in the Bronx, and every day I showed up to our morning kickball game wearing short shorts, a thin cotton T-shirt, and a flimsy, gold-colored scarf tied in a neat bow directly under my chin. (I had plucked it from my mother's collection.) Although it was not a Chanel, it was in the same general fancy family. I was well aware that Adidas shorts and primary color Hanes cotton tees didn't go well with gold lamé scarves, and I did not appreciate the looks I received from fellow campers. And despite its softness, having a thin piece of material tightly wound around my larynx was highly uncomfortable, especially in the heat. I also knew I wasn't a forty-year-old woman attending a brunch. But the thought of exposing my neck in public was simply unbearable, for reasons I cannot fully explain.

Every morning when she saw my outfit, Mom groaned, but never said a word. She probably assumed I was experimenting with fashion and didn't want to discourage me. But by the third week of camp, a quiet female counselor with sweet rosy cheeks made a remark.

"Wendy, I notice you wear scarves every day. The same scarf, actually. How come?"

"I just don't like my neck open to things."

"Oh."

"How can you possibly stand having your neck all open like that?" I asked.

"I . . . I don't know. It doesn't bother me, I guess."

Then it hit me. It *really* didn't bother her. It didn't bother *anyone*. I longed for the good ol' days when life was simple, scarfless—before I had spiraled into a whirlwind of lunacy thanks to *E.T.*

As soon as the summer came to an end, I saw a commercial on TV for Nair, and neck-covering was mysteriously replaced with a burning desire to remove all the hair on my forearms. Somewhere along the way, I had developed an intense yearning to touch smooth surfaces (like my grandparents' marble chess board or the cold metal counter at the bank). I wasn't particularly hairy, but figured that hairless forearms would provide two easily accessible smooth surface options. A few days after seeing the commercial, I somehow managed to get my mother to purchase the product at the supermarket when she wasn't looking, and headed straight to Maya's house for a playdate.

Although Maya could not relate to my longing for hairless arms, she was completely supportive. With her mom safely in the other room, she promptly retrieved a blue towel from the closet and spread it across her bathroom floor. Together we read the instructions on the box, covered my arms in the pungent-smelling cream, and sat on the ground waiting for it to take effect. When we removed the layers of goop and hair with toilet paper, my arms appeared completely hair-free (aside from a tiny area by my right wrist), and from the waist up I looked like a swimmer without any of the muscles.

I luxuriated in the shiny silkiness until I unexpectedly found stubble two days later. Maya asked her babysitter for advice and learned that I'd have to Nair almost every day in order to keep my forearms up to par. I decided I wasn't patient enough for the daily fifteen-minute time commitment, but for weeks I had to avoid wearing long-sleeved shirts to air-conditioned stores because it agitated the natural direction of hair growth. Luckily, though, my hair was light brown, so no one seemed to notice the five-o'clock shadow.

Because I knew that *E.T.* had instigated these behaviors, I was sure that any similarly disturbing movie or TV show would only exacerbate them. This meant that I could not watch films like *Stand By Me*, which, although about a sweet group of boys my age, supposedly included a scene with leeches and a shot of a dead person with his eyes open. I also had to actively avoid

Little House on the Prairie because I had heard that one of the daughters had apparently turned blind and another had once fallen down a well.

Although there was always the natural temptation to view disturbing images, especially in the company of peers, I maturely looked away or left the room whenever creepy, minor musical chords would begin to play. I even stood firm one Friday night at my friend Jessica's massive eighth birthday sleepover when we were informed that the main event of the evening would be a viewing of *Poltergeist*. I hadn't heard of the movie, but the word "poltergeist" sounded haunting. There was no way it was the title of a romantic comedy. I took her mother aside and said, "Look. I have a feeling this movie is not appropriate for me. I'd like to stay, though. What are my options?" I ended up spending a boring but benign couple of hours in the other room by myself watching *Bells Are Ringing*, a musical from the sixties about telephone operators.

Luckily, within months of my first compulsive outbreak, my disturbing-scene "condition" became known among a tight-knit community of mothers. So if I were ever on a playdate at one of their houses, movie and TV watching was strictly monitored for my protection. Like once, at Soomee's tenth birthday gathering, twenty of us were sitting on beanbag chairs, eating triangular tuna sandwiches, when Weird Al Yankovic's new *Eat It* video came on. Soomee's mother rushed in and yelled, "Wendy, please leave the room for two minutes! NOW!" Although slightly alarmed, I followed her instructions without protest. She later explained that at the end of the video Weird Al's eyes turn bright, frighteningly yellow. It was a close call, and I was thankful that Soomee's mother was so on the ball. Witnessing that scene probably would have led to a long and inconvenient bout of eye-checking.

* * *

The rituals and tics continued until fifth grade, when, one Wednesday after school, I happened to flip to an *Oprah* episode featuring a panel of people with severe obsessive-compulsive disorder. One guy spent so much time in his office's executive washroom rinsing his hands that he'd been fired from his job in marketing. He wasn't lazy or incompetent, he just couldn't resist getting up during important meetings to wash his hands just *one more time*. One woman could barely leave her house because she couldn't stop checking to see if the stove was left on, even though she hadn't cooked in weeks. I related. I was immensely relieved to learn that other people out there had strange behaviors like mine, and that our freakishness was legit enough to warrant an episode of *Oprah*.

After each person told his or her story, a short, nebbishy psychiatrist explained that these rituals were manifestations of fears and, like everyday superstitions, helped individuals to feel more in control of their environments. I nodded knowingly. He then suggested a form of cognitive therapy in which patients were directed to do everything in their power to resist their urges—the idea being that if you eliminated a ritual and nothing bad happened, you would feel liberated from the need to continue the activity.

Fascinated by the psychology and inspired to become a saner person, that evening, as I passed by the crevice in the paint on my closet door, I fought my instinct to fill the space with my pinky. I did worry something bad might happen, but remembered the therapist's words and proudly continued through the room. That night I sat on the foot of my bed, looked longingly into the eyes of my stuffed animals, and resisted my need to tightly embrace them.

The break from insanity was nice, but short-lived. After two weeks, I found myself needing to open and close the refrigerator door again and again, so that its rubbery lining would press so strongly into the base unit that the intense merging of surfaces would make me shiver. And every time I read a book for school, even if I was tired and not in the mood, I'd *have* to lick the inner bottom corner of each page to bring out the papery scent, and I'd *have* to stick my nose as far into the bound spine as possible to get enough of a pleasant hit.

Things have been pretty much the same ever since.

Nowadays, I don't feel compelled to check under my bed because I purposely keep my mattress directly on the ground. (Amos doesn't mind.) I do, however, have to wash my hands several times a day—but not because of germs. I simply need to feel the sensation of lukewarm water between my knuckles. Sometimes, to spice things up, I pretend I'm scrubbing in for heart surgery. I wash my hands, turn off the faucet with my elbow, and extend my arms in front of me at right angles. For a few minutes I feel really, really important.

And instead of touching smooth surfaces, I've become obsessed with softness. It's a borderline Lennie from *Of Mice and Men* situation. Suede entices me most because of its alternate light and dark tones. Occasionally, I'll be standing near someone wearing a suede coat and the suede will be uniformly combed in the same direction. I just *have* to lean over and gently run my finger in a line against the grain.

Last month, during a shopping trip to Macy's, I reached out and stroked a massive feathery boa on an older woman standing next to me in the makeup department. Feeling a slight tug, she turned and gave me the meanest glare. I felt bad that I'd invaded her space, but she really had it coming. You can't tempt people by flouncing around in a large fluffy thing like that and expect them not to partake.

Fundamentally, I guess I enjoy living in a perpetual state of sensory overload. But it takes every ounce of self-control to resist licking those cantaloupe-scented Body Shop bath soaps. And it can even be hard to hang out with friends. My friends can be so fun, I just can't *deal* sometimes. I can't love them *enough*. I mean, at least with a cool boyfriend you can just have a lot of sex and get a temporary sense of relief. What are you supposed to do with your friends? I end up smothering them in kisses until they feel totally grossed out. Or try to squeeze them until they burst.

Occasionally, all the affection can get out of hand. My former boss recently told me, "Wendy, I'm starting to doubt your sincerity. You shower my child with the same amount of adoration you give the plastic spoon from Baskin-Robbins." But I *love* that little pink sample spoon. It's so darn . . . concise.

Although I'm still unable to look at images of E.T. without feeling the urge to vomit, and I have yet to watch *Stand By Me*, last month, I did put to rest some of my initial OCD-inspired fears. On a trip to New York to see my mom, I decided to visit a high school friend who works at Kaufman Astoria Studios, which happens to be where *Sesame Street* is filmed. As soon as I entered the massive building, I found my way onto the set of my favorite childhood show. There was no security, and none of the crew seemed to mind, so I kept walking until I found an elephant-like creature being fluffed by wardrobe. Although I was completely starstruck, I mustered up the courage to pat him gently on his side. Feeling the very real celebrity fur of Snuffleupagus between my fingers was more medicinal than a heavy dose of Prozac.

a day in the life of a spero hydra

The hydra is a microscopic life-form that lives at the bottom of ponds and clings to the same small stone for most of its life. It reproduces asexually through a process called budding, and must jiggle carefully along its chosen stone with a mini version of itself attached to its side. I remember learning about the hydra in fourth grade, thinking about my mother, our house, and our daily, unchanging routine, and mumbling, "Huh. That's kinda like my family." I began to view Mom and me as a similar organism—the Spero hydra.

The Spero hydra has a consistent manner of dress:

Every morning Mom and I scurry around the rectangular area of my bedroom in our underwear in an attempt to put together decent outfits.

"WENDY! Did you touch the pile of clothes on your robot toy? You are never to touch my clothes!!! I had a very specific versatile blouse in that pile."

"MAAA! Where are my kneesocks? They're GONE! They were lost in the laundry!!"

Ten seconds later, when each of us finds our items, we silently slide into them with a mutual understanding that our outbursts never happened.

Mom eventually appears in uniform, ready to rumble. She sports a sheer blouse (with built-in shoulder pads); a fitted black knit blazer; a black knit, tailored, knee-length skirt; her recently hand-washed nude control-top stockings; and black pumps. In addition to the required blue-and-green kilt that makes up my school uniform, I insist on wearing my blue-and-green tasseled barrettes, red kneesocks, a white blouse with a turned up Peter Pan collar, my thick brown belt, and my soft, long, navy blue cardigan embroidered with red beads. I am a recognizable figure.

I know this only because on Halloween, my teacher, Mrs. Sherman, goes *as me.*

It might be viewed as inappropriate for a teacher to dress up as a student, but she is one of my favorite teachers and I take it as a huge compliment.

The Spero hydra always attempts a morning meal:

Mom and I squeeze into our tiny kitchen, and she prepares small bowls of Total cereal on the counter next to wrinkly take-out menus, a broken answering machine, and a Ziploc baggie full of pennies.

I am not allowed sugared cereal of any kind because Mom says it is chock-full of chemicals, but knowing I'll get to eat Cocoa Krispies at one of my friend's houses over the weekend, I patiently balance myself on a thin wooden bar stool and break the grainy flakes with my Snoopy spoon. I'm trying to get them soaked and soggy so they can be mashed around into appetizing little piles. Mom does exactly the same thing to her cereal, but standing up. She also digs chunks out of half a grapefruit, inevitably squirting both of us in the eye with citric acid.

The rind and leftover flakes are dumped into a very small, plastic baggie that has been neatly spread out inside a five-inch-tall antique wicker basket the size of a football. Perched next to the cutting board by the sink, it is something one might buy at a quaint country store to hold potpourri. But it is our garbage can.

Because the basket can only hold one or two small discarded items at a time, the baggie needs to be replaced after every meal and brought to the incinerator of the building on our way out. Luckily, we generally only eat very small portions, but in the unlikely event that we finish, say, a quart-sized container of milk, the empty carton has to be placed by the toaster to be taken away on its own.

Sometimes when I go to my friends' houses I am in awe of the huge garbage bins kept under their kitchen sinks. *They must go weeks without having to take the garbage out.* I enjoy tossing used paper towels into those deep bins and watching the garbage actually travel a bit before touching the bottom. When I ask why we can't have our garbage that way, Mom says that those ridiculous big bins under the sink attract roaches. It occurs to me that exposing food on top of the counter could attract just as many, if not more, roaches, but I defer to Mom's judgment and do not press the issue.

The Spero hydra is a slow-moving organism, hesitant to leave its environment:

My nagging to hurry up can barely be heard over the clanking of Mom's Clinique makeup routine in the small living-room bathroom. Trying to convince herself that she is totally on schedule, she meticulously applies a plum-red lip liner with a thin moist brush while attempting to holler, "Wendaay, are you all ready? I'm ready to go . . . We're leaving . . . We are leaving . . . Lemme just . . . One more daaaab . . . We are . . . Out the door . . . We are incredibly out the door . . ."

Bored and anxious to leave, I move into the living room, insert the lower half of my body in between the cushion and side post of the tan love seat, and stare at the ten black garbage bags of clothes lined up next to the dark wood liquor cabinet. They are permanently waiting to be given to the Salvation Army.

If it is a Monday, the day Aida usually comes, Mom screams, "OHMIGOD! MONDAY! WENDY! CLEAN UP!" She frantically organizes her papers on the dining room table, takes out her "DO NOT TOUCH" Post-it notes, and puts them on top of sectioned piles. Then we rush into the bedroom to remove our clothes from the floor.

It is absolutely essential to clean the apartment as much as humanly possible for the housekeeper.

Somehow we eventually make it out of the apartment, into the hallway, and down the elevator to the lobby. I grill her about when exactly she'll be home from work that evening. "Around 10:00 p.m. is meaningless, Mom. 10:00 p.m. or 10:15 p.m.? If you had to guess right now would you say 10:00 p.m. or 10:10 p.m. or 10:15 p.m.? *Just* if you had to guess . . ."

Because she walks far too slowly in her pumps, I pull her arm with all my might down the long, shiny, marble-looking walkway to the double doors of our building. Charlie, the tall, bearded doorman, hollers, "Morning Wendy, morning Mrs. Spero!" Then she writes him a check in exchange for a small wad of cash. This is in the early eighties before ATMs, so everyone gets their dough from Charlie.

Charlie opens the door for us and we march up the walkway of a steep, wide driveway leading to the street—the kind you see in front of fancy hotels. There is scaffolding overhead because the terraces of the building are constantly being remodeled.

We burst out of the nest and into the Upper East Side, a relatively conservative, relatively safe, very yuppie section of the city. As risk factors go, it is a mere extension of the nest.

The Spero hydra is careful when traveling outside its natural environment:

Mom never ever ventures beyond the Upper East Side. She believes that other neighborhoods, particularly ones *downtown* (the Village, Chelsea, even SoHo) are highly precarious—she once had her purse stolen downtown, outside of a French café.

Plus, the streets aren't numbered downtown, so it's just a wild maze and you can easily get lost and find yourself alone on Hudson Street, with no one to ask for help. And taking a cab too far out of our safety zone is expensive, and *no way* will she use the subway, where trains crash and kill hundreds of passengers—she's seen that happen on the news every few years. She's also heard of homeless drunks shoving innocent victims onto the tracks and sneaky female gangsters using scissors to cut the straps of women's purses in order to steal their money and identities.

Mom also says that, regardless of what part of town you're in, you should never *ever* walk down narrow side streets. They are just not crowded enough. You should only walk along main thoroughfares and avenues peppered with stores. (The upper part of New York City is a grid, and we live on Ninetieth Street and First Avenue. If we ever have to go to Ninetieth Street and Third Avenue, Mom makes us walk way out of the way down to Eighty-sixth Street, a main two-way street with lots of shops and restaurants, over to Third Avenue, and then back up to Ninetieth.)

And while Mom considers taxis to be the safest form of daytime transportation, the most dangerous thing you could ever possibly do is take a solo taxi ride after 9 p.m. Instead, you have to take a prearranged *car service* with a well-paid driver. I assume this means that the yellow taxi drivers bustling through the streets during the day "go bad" after dark.

The Spero hydra bisects itself daily:

After traveling the ten blocks to my school, Mom drops me off in front of the building, but not before we engage in a torturous good-bye ritual involving a lot of puckered-lip pecking and Eskimo nose-kissing. She tells me to be extra careful of germs because a stomach bug is probably going around. Then she rushes off in the hopes of getting to her nearby office on time so that, as a social worker, she can help paranoid people all day.

Foreign organisms care for the bisected attachment while the host hydra is away:

Like many of the kids in my class, I get picked up from school by a nanny of some sort.

On Mondays, Aida comes. She gives me a bath at 4:30 p.m., combs knots out of my shoulder-length hair (without the help of conditioner) at 5:00 p.m., and serves broiled Cornish game hen and a slightly salted, steamed green vegetable at 5:30 p.m. on the dot.

If a friend is over, sorry, they'll just have to sit in the other room and amuse themselves while I am cleaned like a dog in the tub. If the friend stays for dinner, we sit at the counter and eat in silence because, according to Aida, talking could cause us to choke on a pea and die. Unfortunately, eating in silence induces laughing fits and the more she yells, "STOP LAUGHING!" the less we can restrain ourselves. She inevitably separates us completely and we eat our dinner in separate rooms. This strikes us as even more amusing.

Tuesday through Friday, a miscellaneous babysitter arrives— whoever is working with us at the time. Most are referrals from friends of friends. For a long while there is Helen, a loud

Trinidadian model who loves showing me her black-and-white headshots. After Helen, there is a small Asian woman in her early twenties who never speaks except to ask me if I am "bored to death by her presence." I think she is followed by a girl named Julia who has a severely broken, perpetually bloody nose, but that could have been a dream.

The bisected attachment worries for the host hydra's safety:

Regardless of which nanny or babysitter is watching over me, around 9 p.m. I become incapable of conversation because my entire body fills with the excruciating anticipation of my mother's return home. She always calls first, so I sit on a brown ottoman gripping the beige phone on my lap, trying to untwist the mangled cord, worried that its knots and contortions might impede the croaky ring from coming through. Every couple of seconds I lift the receiver to make sure there is a dial tone, and then slam it down, praying she didn't call during that split second. Even though we thankfully do not live *downtown*, where things are 100 percent filthy and unsafe, Mom has led me to believe that night is a dangerous time for the entire city because a downtown-*based* psycho could have traveled uptown during the day. One could be lurking behind a lamppost, and, when the time is right, pounce and brutally murder you. You just *never* know. So there is no guarantee that Mom won't get captured near her uptown office by a Downtown Person.

Never for a second do I consider Mom purposely abandoning me, but what if she gets mysteriously sucked into the big world and disappears like a kid on the back of a milk carton? I would become an *orphan*. Even though I hardly notice that I don't have a dad, I do think, *God, it's pretty sketchy that I don't have a backup.*

Mom says that if, God forbid, anything bad ever happens to her, I'm all set to be legally adopted by my friend Jessica's parents. I agree that they are very loving and could easily fit another kid into their big apartment in an emergency, but I simply couldn't live without Mom, end of story. However, sometimes when I'm really bothered by something she does, like wrinkling her upper lip in an unappealing way when she's chewing her Total cereal, I do fantasize for a split second about gabbing with sisters at a dinner table and lounging in an ultra-clean, multi-roomed apartment. With a huge garbage can.

At around 9:45, the handset of our phone eventually lets out a faint buzz-like ring, temporarily putting me out of my misery.

Mom says, "I'm on my way home. See you very soon."

"How soon, Mom?"

"I'm leaving right now. I'm no more than ten minutes away."

"You're not taking the side streets, though, right?"

"Of course not, honey. I'll see you in ten minutes."

Waiting for her arrival is pure torture. As soon as we hang up, I bolt over to our terrace door and grip the off-white curtains, frantically surveying the city streets for a petite Mom-like figure.

After ten or fifteen agonizing minutes, the babysitter lets me go down to the lobby where I pace in my Garfield nightgown, ranting about the dangers of the city to the balding night doorman who doesn't speak English.

"It's pretty safe around here, no? I mean, you haven't seen any downtownish people, right?"

"Yees," says the man as he sits on a stool by the door, twirling a set of keys.

"I mean, I just don't know why it's taking this long. She called and said she was leaving immediately. Do you see anyone coming down the driveway?"

"No," he says, handing me two saltines from behind the desk. "I just hate it when she does this." I munch on the cracker and try to smile. "If she had just said she was coming home after 10 p.m. I wouldn't be worried. But she said she'd come home *before* 10 p.m. She is never good with time."

"Hmm." His warm smile and dimples are slightly comforting.

Finally, when the doorman and I spot the long-awaited image of Mom coming over the hill of the driveway, we share a sigh of relief.

The host hydra attempts an evening meal:

As soon as she pays the babysitter, who quickly shuffles out the door, Mom nibbles on dinner *while* listening to me complain about feeling left out during recess *while* proofreading my book report *while* checking my math homework.

Her meal usually consists of half a Cornish game hen that she glazed with strawberry jam over the weekend. We cannot go a day without sweetly glazed hen. Red meat isn't good for cholesterol levels and both of us agree that steamed fish filets, which are of course good for you, taste too—fishy. She also prepares a compact Greek salad and eats it out of a massive wooden salad bowl that other grown-ups might use for a crowded dinner party.

Sometimes, Mom will also nibble on a mini pita pocket. Pita is the only bread product ever allowed in our house. On the rare occasions that she lets me have a hamburger, it's barely enjoyable because it's served on a thin, stiff pita. Melting cheese on pita is encouraged, but it had better be a fancy gourmet kind, like sharp cheddar or Edam. Processed cheese is full of bad substances and strictly forbidden.

Mom's dinner is cold because she hasn't eaten since lunch

and there is just no time for heating up. We eventually get a microwave installed above the stove, but she doesn't know how to use it, and even when it's off she ducks when passing by to avoid any potentially harmful electromagnetic waves.

The host hydra may encounter conflict with its attachment:

As Mom hurriedly chews, I scream at the top of my lungs and throw an antique chair or two across the living room. Her suggestions aren't fixing the multiplication problems on my assignment sheet! Her therapist approach—"Wendaay, honey, let's sit down and talk about the problem, oookay?"—makes me want to cause MAJOR DESTRUCTION. Panting with fury, I worry that I actually resemble the crazy mother in *Mommy Dearest*, the one and only disturbing movie I couldn't resist watching one Tuesday evening. Even though I have never thrown a hanger, I feel deeply guilty about being a potentially abusive *daughter*. This makes me feel resentful. So as my mother talks to me about "getting a better handle on my anger," I decide to slam each door in the house about five times—each swing more explosive than the next. Cracks are left in the doorframes.

Temper tantrums eventually get boring, so while Mom is busy trying to get organized, I sneak into the kitchen and serve myself a small bowl of coffee-flavored Häagen-Dazs ice cream or a couple of Pepperidge Farm Mint Milano cookies. I would prefer cooler brands, but Mom won't let me have Chips Ahoy or Good Humor because, unlike Häagen-Dazs and Pepperidge Farm, they are chemically enhanced.

Mom eventually asks me to please go to my room and to keep the door shut so she can make some work phone calls. I take the food into the bedroom but inevitably emerge and tiptoe to the kitchen to get more. Mom squints her eyebrows together, turns red, and points to my door, worried that at any moment I'll make a sound that would allow her clients to discover she's making a call from a real three-dimensional environment.

The Spero hydra enjoys evening recreation:

When her work calls are finished, Mom and I sit on the sofa in the living room and watch the end of *Thirtysomething* or *LA Law* on a small, eight-inch TV squeezed into a lower shelf on the bookcase. The TV is half obstructed by phone and answering machine cords, most of which aren't attached to actual contraptions anymore but have somehow gotten entwined in a mass over the years.

The Spero hydra's environment faces dangers:

Crisis Scenario 1

We find a HUGE mutant roach by the vent in the living room bathroom. It is not of this earth.

It has a *face*.

With an *expression*.

We see the monster simultaneously, scream bloody murder and run around in circles with our arms waving in helplessness.

Mom's like, "Okay. Breathe. Wendaay . . . I'm getting help." I sit whimpering on the piano bench and she gets on the intercom to talk to the doorman. "Sir, there is a bug in apartment 7D, and I need you to address this."

"Uh, no leave door. No."

"Sir, I don't think you understand how dire this is. This is *dire*. Look, I will man the door! *I* will guard the building from intruders!"

He won't budge. So she calls the fire department.

"Hi—I'm so sorry, um, this is *not* an emergency . . . this is not *fire* related . . . but, I was *wondering* . . . if you had time . . . if you could send just one man to kill . . . a very large bug. Certainly don't dispatch a truck, I will provide money for a cab. Uh huh. Okay. Very good."

She hangs up and mumbles, "Yeah, they don't do that." Half crying and half hysterically laughing, we shut the door to the bathroom, blockade the space between the door and the floor with bath towels, and whimper until morning when the super can come.

Crisis Scenario 2

I complain of a strange smell coming from the heater. We stick our noses up to the metal bars and conclude that something inside has definitely become overly heated. Mom calls down to the doorman who says he can't leave his post.

So she calls the fire department.

"Yes, hi—there's a funny smell in my heater, maybe something was burned . . ."

She is in mid-sentence when the loudest sirens ever come screaming down the avenue. She puts her hand over the receiver and whispers, "Do you hear that, Wendaay? Oh God, there must be a horrible fire somewhere. I hope the people are okay."

A second later, I hear pounding on our front door.

"THIS IS THE FIRE DEPARTMENT. OPEN UP!"

I unfasten the lock to find ten huge men in full-on fire gear.

Mom is still on the phone with the fire department. "No, I don't think it's a fire *per se*, but there is something weird about it."

The firemen barge through the door and rush into the living room. Mom turns around totally confused. "What? I'm talking on the phone with the fire department *right* now. This is just wild."

"Ma'am, we're just doing our job. Where's the source of the problem?"

We lead them toward the heater, where they take apart the metal covering and find the little horseman from Monopoly, unharmed.

The Spero hydra has nocturnal rituals:

Around midnight, Mom goes to the master bathroom and makes monkey-like grunting noises in front of the mirror. Her friend has told her that doing facial exercises while making long vowel sounds will reduce wrinkles. I think Mom is the most beautiful person in the world and wish she wouldn't do anything that could change her appearance.

After she tucks me into my trundle bed and we exchange thirty-five "I love you's," Mom goes into the living room and, as if she is preparing a bed for a guest, removes the pillows from the couch, yanks the heavy metal bar in the center, unfolds the contraption into a twin-sized mattress, and starts to make it up with sheets that have been folded up in a nearby closet since morning.

Then, in between checking under the bed for aliens, we share a few more rounds of affection through the wall.

"I LOVE YOU MOM!"

"I LOVE YOU TOO, DEAR!"

"I LOVE YOU, THOUGH, MOM!"

"OK, I LOVE YOU TOO, DEAR. GO TO BED NOW."

Because everyone knows that sleeping with the heat on can cause a sore throat, and because my mother has never been motivated to buy a proper down comforter for herself, when I wander into the living room ten minutes later, I find a pile of ten to twelve doubled-over cotton blankets topped with a small, pink down jacket (the sleeves tied together for extra layering), which resembles a crushed cherry at the summit of a tall, messy, melting sundae. The lump at the very bottom is my mother, her petite nose and eyes peeping out by her nearby desk lamp, which is very dim because one of the two bulbs has burned out. She strains toward the faint light source trying to muster up enough energy to continue reading the marriage announcement section of the *New York Times*.

I am coming in to give her yet another hug and to hunt under all those covers for her soft rosy cheeks and gently press them in with my index finger, like I do with white rolls in supermarkets. I beg to sleep with her and once she gives in I carefully slide underneath the layers and make sure that the little pink down jacket at the top remains in place. We cling ourselves to sleep.

Years later, after eventually leaving its hydra host, the attachment retains parasitic tendencies:

I talk to my mother on the phone from my L.A. apartment. Our connection is crackly because she still has the same overly knotty phone cord. I tell her I am writing about our routine on Ninetieth and First Avenue. She says, "Wendaay, you can talk about me in your book but I feel very *uncomfortable* with you just . . . *announcing* that you grew up on Ninetieth and First."

"Why?"

"You never know. You just never *ever* know."

* * *

I didn't actually grow up on Ninetieth and First. My mom just *really* didn't want me to tell you where we lived. So I changed it.
'Cause you never know.

me, mom, and him

A mysterious, abstract, porcelain sculpture has always sat on the top shelf of my mother's bookcase, sandwiched between a thick book entitled *Sex for One: The Joy of Self-loving* and the instructional manual *To Be a Jew*. The figure consists of a smooth round ball placed inside a hollow ovular structure the size of a basketball. One Saturday night when I was five, my mom was hosting a small dinner party, and some dude with a lot of hair poking out of his ears came up to me, pointed to the sculpture, and said, "I made that in graduate school. Do you know what it's supposed to be, honey? That is you and your mother as one. Powerful stuff. It's you crouching as you resist emerging from the opening of her warm uterus." I almost barfed.

I never stopped thinking that the guy was a major lame-o for creating such a cheesy piece of "art" or for making an inappropriately frank comment about my mother's deep vaginal cavity. But after a few weeks, I secretly liked the idea of there being a tangible grown-up item in the house that might remind my mother of our solidarity as a team, and the fact that there was simply no need or room in our lives for a potential father character who would surely spoil our shtick.

Every time my mother prepared for her monthly, Saturday-night blind date, I'd wonder why she needed to look outside of our relationship for companionship. One time, while she was inserting shoulder pads into a long floral dress, I marched up to her and said, "Mom, really, there is nothing a man can give you that I can't. Am I not enough?" She replied that sometimes parents need to socialize with other grown-ups, and that her need for a relationship with a man did not mean that anything was lacking between us. It seemed like she was giving me a line. But then she added, "And don't you want a father? It could be fun to have a man around sometimes, no? Maybe you would feel less worried about me, too."

She almost had a point, I thought. Sometimes I was overwhelmed by concern for my mother's safety, and it might be reassuring to share the angst with another person. And yes, a father might be fun if he could pick me up and swing me around, like some of my friends' fathers did. Unlike my mother, fathers also wore pants, and that would allow them to sit on the floor with you when playing board games. (My mom only wore knit skirts, so when we played board games together, I'd sit on the rug and she'd sit on an antique chair and awkwardly reach down when it was her turn to move a piece. It was so not-as-fun that way.)

But no. Those potential advantages did not outweigh the risk of sharing my mother with someone else. She was too good to share, and frankly, there wasn't that much of her to go around. Not only was she physically tiny, but her downtime was precious and infrequent. And, our one-on-one dynamic was key. I won most of our fights, or at least I thought I did, and when it came down to it, I could usually squirm my way out of a punishment. If there was a second parent around, it would be two against one, and God knows what kind of order that could put into motion.

Plus, not having a father made me feel more unique. While all the kids at school created Father's Day cards, I'd get special attention. "Wendy, why don't you make a collage for your grandfather or . . . your uncle?" When peers asked me what I was doing for Father's Day, I'd say "nothing" and they'd instantly remember my "circumstance" and apologize. I felt a little like I was getting credit for something I didn't do. A stepfather would put me in the category of every other kid I knew with divorced and remarried parents.

Despite my well-argued protests and the supposedly powerful symbol on the shelf of me entwined in my mother's warm uterus, Mom continued her search for a man to sweep us both off our feet. Once, at age eight, I was dragged to a single-parent weekend extravaganza at a resort in the Catskills where single-parent families were supposed to meet and fall madly in love, à la *The Brady Bunch*. The organizers, a hippie couple who had met at a similar type of event ten years earlier, set up group activities like balloon tosses and potato sack races. At one point, Mom and I stood across from a kid and his balding middle-aged father, who I think was named Monroe (or at least he looked like a Monroe). The two adults made small talk about their careers while the pudgy boy and I tossed a dripping avocado-sized water balloon back and forth while thinking, *Please don't hit it off. Please don't hit it off. This kid would not be a fun sibling. Please don't hit it off.*

Before the trip, Mom and I agreed that she wouldn't ditch me, so even though there was a decent selection of bachelors and readily available babysitters, she never once went off to mingle on her own. She was even willing to include me in the organized single-parent dinners at night. Every evening, the kids, who ranged from ages five to fifteen, got shipped to a partially lit cafeteria to eat macaroni and cheese, while the adults ate in a glistening dining hall with assigned seats. At my mother's table there were seven men, seven women, and me, my nose resting on the table's surface. I'd listen to her laugh with the men, and would take pleasure in any uncomfortable pauses, which I knew indicated a lack of chemistry.

I remember feeling great respect for my mom during those meals. She wasn't like those other parents who easily discarded their children all willy-nilly.

Luckily, by the end of our Catskills retreat, our family unit remained intact. No unnecessary father figure had been inserted.

Soon after, Jerry, a cuddly bearded man, entered our lives. The first time Jerry came to pick my mother up for dinner, he wisely handed me a large prepackaged chocolate chip cookie. I was not above bribery and was impressed by his strategy. When I looked back at Mom for approval, she smiled. For a split second, I actually considered that the man might bring something to the table: processed food. The possibilities were endless—Chips Ahoy, Kraft singles, Cap'n Crunch, and beyond. I was open to this. Most important, his gesture indicated an understanding of his inferior place in our lives. Unlike the others, he knew that *he* was the one needing to impress *me*, the judgmental daughter with the power to approve or disapprove.

Jerry, however, only lasted two dates. When I asked why he was let go so quickly, Mom said he wasn't all that attractive and was geographically undesirable. He lived upstate or something. But I'm happy to report that his memory has stayed with us. In fact, he soon became our future prototype for "father." For years, if something heavy like a desk or a really thick dictionary needed lifting, I'd say, "If only you had given Jerry more of a chance. Poor, unattractive, geographically undesirable Jerry with the big cookie."

All the power I thought I had over these interlopers went down the toilet after my mother started dating Ron, a major fucking asshole. He was the financial analyst with the nasty space between his two front teeth who was at my house the night I saw *E.T.* He'd say things to me like "Kids should be seen and not heard." When I'd scream back that, in fact, kids should be seen and heard and could teach adults a thing or two, he'd actually go through a list of supposedly proven psychological theories why nine-year-old girls become better women if they just sit quietly and listen instead of barking out opinions. When I'd look to Mom for support she'd say, "Children . . . stop it, now." Not even taking my side.

One Friday evening, Mom suggested that the three of us play a group game of Monopoly. As we set up the board, Ron appointed himself banker and started dealing out an obscene number of fifty and one hundred dollar bills. I said, "Uh, excuse me? Each player is supposed to get two one-hundred-dollar bills, four fifty-dollar bills, six twenties, etc."

"As long as everyone gets the same total amount, it doesn't matter what the bills are," he replied, rolling up the sleeves of his argyle sweater.

"Yes it does. Everyone knows you are supposed to get a certain number of each kind. That is part of the fun of the game!"

"Well I'm not everyone."

"You have to play by the rules of the game!"

"The game is a theoretical construct. We can play it out however we want."

"And I WANT two one hundreds and four fifties!"

"And I don't. And I'm the banker."

I threw the board on the floor, sobbed, and griped for four hours to my five-foot-tall Pink Panther about what a victim I'd become in my mother's romantic pursuits.

Oh, and as if his selfishness wasn't enough, Ron kept numerous large, smelly loafers in my already cluttered room. Also, I saw him bite his toenail once when he thought no one was looking.

Two years later when they finally broke up, Mom actually apologized for her lapse in judgment. He ended up becoming quite a good "get out of jail free card." I'd be like, "Mom, sorry for that pointless, yet loud, temper tantrum I just had in the middle of the freezer section of the supermarket... You did date *Ron*, though." As her guilt came flooding back, I'd be completely exonerated.

My mom went on a blind date with her next real boyfriend, Kevin, the first evening of my freshman year of high school. I was too distracted after my big day to even notice, but soon after, they began formally seeing each other. For the first time I was psyched about her being in a real relationship. As a maturing teenager, I appreciated the fact that he made her happy. More important, I appreciated the fact that he distracted her from spinning out of overprotective control as I attempted a high school social life (which included wearing provocative outfits and taking cabs—past 9 p.m. no less—to unsupervised house parties located on side streets).

Because Kevin lived in Connecticut and they could only see each other on weekends, they talked on the phone every night before falling asleep. This was fine until I started dating the High School Boyfriend and needed to talk to *him* on the phone every night before falling asleep. Mom refused to understand the concept of getting a second line, so every night she'd lay under her many blankets and kiss good-night good-byes into the phone receiver before yelling, "OK WEN! IT'S ALL YOURS

NOW!" I'd then pick up in my room and make what she considered to be the more important call of the evening.

About six months into their relationship, when I first met Kevin's family during a weekend visit to his house, I was alarmed by the striking differences between us and them. One of Kevin's sons was a serious thespian who loved to imagine twists on current movies. As we sat down to dinner he turned to me, grabbed his chin and said, "Picture it. *Braveheart.* Only instead of kilts, all the men are wearing dark jean skirts." His other son was in the midst of finishing a PhD in molecular endocrinology and had spent the day frantically gene splicing. Kevin's brother, a renowned engineer and scientist responsible for the invention of the CAT scan or something, sat across the table from us and started a heated discussion about osmosis. All the men eagerly chimed in as my mother and I sat quietly in the corner—Mom marveling at all the intellect around us, and me counting the minutes until I could escape into his den and watch his *Fletch Lives* video.

For her wedding to Kevin last year (she refused to get married until she felt I was settled enough in my own life), my mom got all giggly and went all out with "save the dates," invitations, a mini-veil, a white dress, and a bouquet. The indulgence could not have been more deserved and endearing. But the whole thing was completely surreal to me. At one point in the ceremony, I made eye contact with my future thespian stepbrother across the pulpit and we could NOT stop laughing. I was shaking so hard I almost lost my grip of the chuppah. My mom was getting *married.* She was in a *wedding dress.* With *extra shoulder pads.*

A part of me was genuinely excited about being part of a larger family. Maybe my stepbrothers and I could bond over our parents' unexplainable shared passion for *10 Things I Hate About*

You, and maybe someday we'd all pile into a station wagon and head to Wally World. A group of five could be a nice change of pace, and I knew our special twosome dynamic would never be truly compromised. But I was still relieved when my mother refused to leave New York City and opted to have a long-distance marriage instead. Every Saturday morning she takes a four-hour bus ride up to Kevin's house, spends quality time with her husband, and returns late Sunday night in time for work. Like me, she can't really move to the country because she doesn't know how to drive, and, like me, she's overly attached to our apartment, which has now become a minefield of old yearbooks, bills, files, reports, and most important, mysterious, tacky female-genitalia art.

an emotional outlet

I've never been particularly good at estimating the number of jelly beans in jars at school fairs, or the age of vaguely wrinkly women wearing hip low-rise jeans, or the gender of androgynous people with shortish curly hair sitting across from me on commuter trains. But I'm gonna take a stab in the dark and say that exactly 36 percent of my life has been spent at discount fashion department stores.

When I was five years old, the Emotional Outlet entered the world with gusto. My mother received a birth announcement in the mail, a glossy pink index card, saying something like "Finally, we're here. Visit us! Top Designers at Discount Prices. Can't wait to meet you." Because it was immediately stuck up on our fridge with a plastic yellow alphabet-letter magnet, I knew that if this baby was really located anywhere near our apartment building, it would only be a matter of weeks before it became a permanent stop in our endless weekend grocery/ cosmetics/prescriptions errand routine.

Sure enough, that Saturday, we paid the first of ten thousand horribly uneventful visits to this torturous establishment, which turned out to be a mere five blocks from our home. It was right next to Chicky's on Eighty-sixth Street, a spicy chicken fast-food restaurant whose curry fumes cleared your sinuses from blocks away.

In the window of the Emotional Outlet was a collection of ultrathin mannequins. Together, they looked like an Evolution of Man exhibit at a natural history museum—only with a midlife-crisis spin. Six women in different poses, each seeming more and more dedicated to covering up her late-forties angst with silky scarves and pin-tucked blazers. Their wrists were bent at forty-five-degree angles, making them seem desperately flippant and carefree.

As we entered through the double doors, a sultry female voice reverberated from a speaker in the ceiling: "Attention, shoppers. There is a special sale on the mezzanine level." *Mezzanine*. Something about the combination of *m* and *z* sounds made me instantly nauseated. Gazing out into the sea of discounted fashions before her, my mother murmured something about my staying no more than a half-inch from her side at all times, and I followed her closely as she pitter-pattered through the wide main room, weaving in and out of the racks dedicated to petites. Every few minutes, she'd hold a garment up while cocking her head to the side and expelling a slight gurgle of potential interest. I did commentary in my head. "This is a close one. There's a lot of consideration. Will the Donna Karan discounted blouse get swung onto the left arm and make it to the next round? It's looking positive . . . almost . . . almost . . . and . . . yes! It's one lucky day for Ms. Frilly Sleeves and one unlucky day for Ms. Wendy who will now be stuck waiting in this loathsome sea of grown-up textiles that much longer." But I mustered up the energy to look on the bright side, which was that the store was relatively small (despite the mezzanine), with only three blouse aisles and one skirt aisle. It was times like these that my mother's unexplained refusal to wear pants was a damn good thing.

Once she loaded up both her arms to capacity, I was dragged

to the dressing room in back. Because there was no space for me in the small changing area behind the drapery, I leaned on the adjacent wall and slowly slid downward, eventually collapsing into a ball as I played with the sharp ridges at the top of my loose front tooth with the tip of my tongue. "Ma'am, your daughter can't sit here like that," said a stocky, heavily made-up saleswoman. "It's better if she sits by the guard." The guard was a manly dude in a uniform who was unhappily serving apple juice in little paper Dixie cups by a bowl of pretzels near the front of the store.

You'd think the refreshments would have seriously improved my predicament, but I knew that juice would only make me have to pee, and I was not a big fan of small, crunchy snacks, even though the sound they made against my back teeth was somewhat pleasing. Plus, the taste of dry nibbly food just reminded me of my mother's friends' holiday parties, which were even more excruciating than discount designer clothing shopping because I'd always get set up with another kid. "I heard there's gonna be another kid there. We'll find a way to introduce you guys!" was the worst possible phrase I could ever hear. At these parties I'd hoist up my itchy party tights, which crept downward and gathered in rolly bunches at my ankles, take my mother's hand, and follow her to the hors d'oeuvres table where the "other kid" was sulking and double dipping carrots into a bean spread. We'd look one another up and down and grunt, "Hey," knowing full well we probably had no toys in common. We'd almost bond about the fact that we could never bond. Then I'd take a dull knife and spend the next hour looking away, surreptitiously digging out all the inner goo of the Brie cheese and molding it into multiple little snowmen, leaving a hollow shell of white crust intact on the plate.

As I flopped into an uncomfortable seat at the front of the

Emotional Outlet, next to the emotionless guard, praying that my mother would dislike all of her picks so we could avoid the checkout line, I rested my nostrils up against the chair's back and experienced the wondrous ripe scent of synthetic upholstered furniture. As I rubbed my nose cartilage back and forth on the smooth surface, two middle-aged men separately approached and sat down next to me. They stared ahead in despair as their wives ran off to "take a quick peek." I shot them a look that said, "I feel your pain." I knew that in a matter of minutes they too would come to realize the awful truth. I had overheard my mom say that the pieces she was planning to try on had "versatility." From my experience, I knew that "versatility" was something grown-up females wanted in their clothes. The Emotional Outlet was here to stay.

Two years or 999 visits or 700,000,002 vinyl chair sniffs later, my mother and I turned the corner at Eighty-sixth Street and saw a blackened dusty cave where her favorite discount store used to stand. After long consultations with other mothers in the neighborhood, Mom deduced that an irrationally dissatisfied customer had used the store as an actual emotional outlet and set it on fire. I was pleased, but the general lack of mournfulness on her part was troubling. It could only mean that she was already considering another discount clothing enterprise to replace the dark emotional void.

Because my mother never left our immediate neighborhood except to go to Bloomingdale's, and because the Emotional Outlet had been the only one of its kind, I no longer had to endure discount designer clothing shopping on a weekly basis. But the subsequent annual visits to Loehmann's, a discount fashion mecca in New Jersey (there wasn't yet a branch in New York City), were just as bad, if not worse.

Every April my mother would need to go over her taxes with

my Uncle Bernie, her brother-in-law and accountant, and because he lived near a Loehmann's, she'd make a mini-vacation
out of it. She'd take off part of a Friday and we'd travel two
hours on the bus in the late afternoon and stay overnight with
Bernie and my mom's older sister, Aunt Irma, in their clean suburban house. They were very nice and asked me a lot of questions about my friends, and sometimes they served salad
dressing from the bottle and processed cheddar cheese spread
on Ritz crackers, delicacies prohibited in our home.

It was the DAYLONG Loehmann's portion of this trip that
was so insufferable. At 8:30 a.m. Saturday morning we'd get up,
pack processed turkey or tuna salad lunches, and load into
Aunt Irma's Volkswagen to beat any possible Loehmann's traffic. Apparently, if you got there past 11:00 a.m., all the great
deals would be gone. As we'd pull into the parking lot, I'd eye
the magnificent Toys "R" Us outlet across the street and drool.
I'd beg, "MOM. This year can we go after? It's RIGHT THERE.
PLEASE?"

"Yes. If we have time afterward," she'd say while blotting her
face with a coat of powder. This obviously meant, "I'm sorry, but
we definitely won't have time because, let's face it, I'm gonna be
here for nine hours."

We'd walk through the metal doors and enter cutthroat,
blood-curdling mayhem. Middle-aged female grunting beasts
of all shapes and sizes would be stabbing one another with
long, red, freshly painted fingernails while racing to dig
through discarded piles of high-quality, severely marked down
items. Feeling very above all the brouhaha, I'd pity their need to
buy boring starchy office garb, and their interest in frequently
using words like *slimming* and *becoming*.

Since there was a likelihood of getting trampled if I followed
my mother through the aisles, she'd allow me to wait in the

massive, communal dressing room. (I was eight or nine then—more trustworthy than I'd been during her Emotional Outlet days—and all the women seemed far too busy sucking in their stomachs to kidnap me.) Every wall of the square, open space was covered in mirrors, and I would sit on a rickety wooden bench in the back, surrounded by pounds of reflected aging cellulite.

All day long, a revolving crowd of thirty to forty half-naked women would parade around and examine their profiles beneath a pungent cloud of Chanel No. 5. Periodically, they'd come together as one and offer brutal, unsolicited advice to one another. "Miss, that color washes you right out. I'd get that in a darker shade. And you should get that in a larger size. You're likely to rip right through it—HEY, DID ANYONE SEE A GREEN, LATE SPRING/EARLY FALL TOP OUT THERE THAT MIGHT GO WITH THESE CULOTTES?"

Many would try on bras for hours on end and I would seize the opportunity to study the divergent array of live bare boobs. The pointier ones were the most frightening because they looked like they could poke your eye out if you accidentally leaned too far forward.

I'd also glance at the dirty gray carpet and search for those sharp plastic twisty things used for attaching price tags. To pass the time, I'd gather as many as possible and sit with a pile on my lap, arranging them into elaborate formations up and down my thigh. Then I'd zone out and push their thin tips under my chewed thumbnail. It hurt. But in a pleasurable way.

Sometimes the dressing room clerks would assemble a full-length, fold-out mirror for people who desired privacy while undressing. It was rarely utilized—part of the overall appeal of Loehmann's, it seemed, was disrobing in a frenzied mob-like manner. So I'd spend at least an hour behind it, pretending to be a Rockette. The mirrors on the right and the left sides created a never-ending echo of identical reflections. I'd lift my knee up and down and marvel at the precision of our performance line, occasionally yelling, "Number 34! You're off!"

Nine exhausting hours later, Aunt Irma would come in and tell me to meet them at the checkout line in five minutes and to grab a few cartons of shoulder pads from the nearby shelf on the way. The shoulder pads were sold in small round boxes that resembled ice cream containers. It was alarming that something as boring as a shoulder pad came inside such delightful packaging.

Upon arriving at the checkout, I'd barely recognize my mother. Not only was she completely buried in clothes and hangers, but a thick, droopy layer of exhaustion covered her face. As she unloaded her purchases onto the counter, she'd mumble rationalizations to me, Irma, and the cashier. "You can never have too many basic black skirts, right? Right? They're versatile. For weekends and the office. And that Anne Klein coat, well, did you feel the thickness? Irma, feel the thickness again. Yeah, black skirts will never go out of style. They are *basic*. You can never have too many, right?"

Irma and the cashier nodded casually, but I nodded emphatically. The more nodding she saw, the more assured she'd feel. This would greatly reduce the chances of indecision or lengthy debate.

"And these are designer clothes," she'd continue, wiping her brow with a tissue. "They are *investments*. I must be saving hundreds of dollars here. *Hundreds!* How much am I saving here?! HOW MUCH?! Miss, seriously, how much am I saving?"

The cashier would dryly reply, "You're saving a lot, miss."

"SEE! I'm saving, Irma. I'm saving."

As we'd pull out of the lot I'd make one last pointless request for Toys "R" Us just for the hell of it. Mom would say, "We're tired, honey, and we've got to beat the Loehmann's traffic going back. If we wait longer we'll get stuck bumper-to-bumper. Next time, dear."

On our sixth Loehmann's anniversary, right after my fourteenth birthday, I was sitting in the dressing room, digging one of those sharp plastic twisty things under my thumbnail, when I spotted a tight, floral, cotton top with a low-cut lace neckline on the rejection rack. A foreign sensation came over me: I found myself wanting to try it on. I was ashamed. I had always taken a strong stand against Loehmann's, and I knew an act like that would definitely hurt my cause. But my mother and aunt were not in sight, so I quickly gave in. After pushing my head through the neckline, I could smell the perfume of the woman who'd just taken it off. I felt connected to something larger than myself.

The top looked totally adorable, but the real rush came once I saw the tag: 75 percent off. Within minutes I became one of the nutso women I'd watched for years from the sidelines. I threw caution to the wind and tried on at least fifty items that day. My mother was ecstatic, and because we were at *Loehmann's*, she insisted we buy everything that fit me. "They're *investments*, honey. These are timeless designer labels. And you can never have enough basic black skirts. And Irma, we're saving hundreds, right? HUNDREDS!"

As we pulled out of the lot that evening, I didn't even notice the Toys "R" Us.

vertical halloweens

Recently, I've been polling my friends, asking where they see themselves living in five to ten years, and their answers are freaking me out. Many of the people I assumed would remain in New York City forever might permanently leave one day to raise children. They say that, cost aside, it would be "almost wrong" for a young kid to be deprived of a dewy, freshly cut lawn or a backyard with a tire swing in favor of growing up *in* the *actual* city amidst all the hustle.

That's just not true.

Now, I'm not saying that I when I visited suburban homes as a young kid I never felt jealous. Once, when my mother and I stayed with her second cousin twice removed in Great Neck, New York, he drove us to a mazelike, football field–sized supermarket. My local supermarket was maybe one thirty-second of its magnitude. I'd never seen such a long candy aisle, or a bag of sugar that was as big as a chubby baby. When we loaded the car with an impressive twenty-four-pack of quilted toilet paper, all I could think about for days was how my cousin got all those rolls home in one fell swoop. My mother and I would have had to make at least ten trips to the market to reach that kind of quantity, and even then, there'd be no place to store such an exciting amount. We could barely hold a four-pack. We'd have to split it up and squeeze two spare rolls under the bathroom sink and one behind the toilet.

And there was my Aunt Cynthia's suburban house, also on Long Island, where I was actually *encouraged* to leave food on my plate when I put it in the sink. She had a garbage disposal that would simply suck your leftovers away. I would purposely pile on extra helpings during dinner, just so I could watch the remains be crushed into nothingness. In Manhattan, if you wash a dish and mere bits of lettuce get in the drain, you are seriously doomed. The whole system will get clogged, and the super will never show up, and a foul lettuce-smelling liquid will drip into the corners of the kitchen, and, despite the use of Combat pest killer and frequent visits from exterminators, various-sized roaches will surely invade and give you and your family a nervous breakdown.

And nothing was better than coming out of a shower in a towel in a suburban home and making your way through the soft wool threads of wall-to-wall carpeting. My apartment (and most of my friends' apartments) had cold, hardwood floors and a few itchy rugs. When I was young and visited Aunt Irma's house for our annual Loehmann's excursion, it was an utter joy to feel softness between my toes and ever-so-slightly sink into the ground with every step. And I loved hiding my Smurfs from Gargamel in the long strands, imagining them hiking through a tall cornfield.

Also, the fact that people had a personal set of stairs *in their house* never ceased to amaze me. At any time they could sit on them comfortably with their knees folded inward and watch a Slinky meander its way downward. My Slinky had nowhere to walk. It could only make one pathetic journey from a low chair to the floor.

HOWEVER.

I was always relieved to return to the city.

I didn't have a dewy, freshly cut lawn or a backyard with a tire swing. But I did have a fantastically long and narrow hallway outside of my apartment door that went straight for several yards and then turned a dramatic corner. The hallway was carpeted with a thin, scratchy, orange-colored material, but if you wore thick socks, you could experience decent amounts of give beneath your feet. "Playing in the hall" with friends who came over proved to be an enjoyable year-round activity. Rain or shine, we would keep my front door unlocked and saunter into the narrow space. (If it's raining in the suburbs, aren't kids forced to sit by the windowsill and start a thousand-piece puzzle of a basket of kittens? Or to go into the basement and spend the afternoon desperately trying to find that old *National Geographic* with the nude natives in it?)

Sometimes friends and I would throw a reddish rubber ball the size of a globe from one side of the hall to the next. Safely surrounded by a ceiling and walls, we'd never have to deal with the ball getting stuck in a suburban tree or going across a suburban street or rolling under a suburban parked car. The hall was one large pinball machine. The neighbors never seemed to mind the thumping and squealing, except when the ball banged directly against their door. But because they had to unlock four bolts and a safety chain in order to come out and complain, we had plenty of time to scurry back into the apartment to avoid confrontation.

For the most part, I didn't know our neighbors very well, but putting our ears to their doors and trying to decipher snippets of marital disagreements was a nice way for my friends and me to break up the hallway games. "LARRY, I'm just sick of it!" "Lower your voice, Gloria." "NO! WHY SHOULDN'T EVERYONE KNOW THAT YOUR GODDAMN SNORING IS

TEARING US APART! WHY SHOULD I BE QUIET WHEN YOU SNORE JUST AS LOUD?" It can't be nearly as easy for a kid to eavesdrop in the suburbs.

My friends and I often brought snacks into the hall, with no danger of encountering a swarm of suburban insects. A tall black tubular ashtray stood between the two elevators, and my friends and I enjoyed throwing raisins from various distances into the round tin on top.

Once, when I was eight years old, my friend Sara, who lived a couple of blocks away, got bored of throwing raisins into the ashtray and decided instead to pull down her pants and pee in it. I was privately disturbed by this for weeks, worried the waste would somehow seep into the floorboards, become toxic, and spread a rare disease. So, okay, a point for the suburbs. Peeing in a yard probably wouldn't pose such a problem.

(Sara was one of those overtly spoiled girls who loved being daring and irresponsible and had no real appreciation of her elaborate sticker collection. She had a lot of quality smellies, puffies, and oilies, which she messily stuck DIRECTLY to the pages of her sticker book. Any real sticker trader knew that you were supposed to keep the backs on your stickers and just lay them tightly in place behind the clear plastic flap of the album. This allowed for easy removal during bargaining. It was the lack of appreciation for this important sticker process that kept me at an arm's length from Sara. The peeing incident only confirmed that we were on totally different wavelengths.)

Fun could also be had in the building elevators. The buttons inside were *heat activated*, like an appliance on *The Jetsons*. Lighting up rows of buttons with a puff of hot hair from my mouth was remarkably rewarding. My breath felt magical. Once a month my mother and I would get in the elevator and find twenty buttons lit up because some other kid in the building had done the whole hot-breathing thing. We'd have to stop at every floor, but I'd think, *Good for them.*

I also found it fascinating to see how the elevator buttons in my friends' buildings were arranged (vertically or horizontally) and whether or not they included the number thirteen. My building didn't have a thirteen. It obviously had a thirteenth floor, but in the elevator it was called fourteen. I was, and still am impressed when a building fully acknowledges the thirteenth floor by listing it by its real name. Way to ignore society's silly superstitions. I'd never live on thirteen, but God bless those freaks who want to risk it.

The elevators and long hallways of many Manhattan apartment buildings were the most enjoyable on Halloween. Just like many suburban kids, I loved plotting my costume months in advance, eventually dressing up as a bum or a Jolly Rancher or an eggplant. And if I ran out of time to make my own truly original costume, I loved the comforting smell of those round, plastic premade masks my mother would let me get—Kermit or Raggedy Ann or Darth Vader (even though I had never seen or barely heard of *Star Wars*). I loved the thin elastic band that held those masks on my head, and how the mouth portion got slightly sticky, and how I'd feel nearly suffocated by the fog of my candy-scented breath. But for me, the best part of Halloween was sliding down the hallways of apartment buildings, riding up and down elevators, and ringing doorbells—all while wearing *socks*. In New York City, you don't have to walk outside and ruin a perfectly put-together Crest toothpaste costume with a clunky pair of penny loafers or blue striped Treatorns. Plus, visible socks added a great final touch to a costume. If you were going as a tomato and wore bright red ankle socks, you were unstoppable.

It was also liberating to not be cold on this most important holiday. We got to enjoy all the greatness of fall—the crispness in the air, the sudden need for hot chocolate, the playing with leaves (Central Park provided more crunchy leaves than any backyard ever could)—but the trick-or-treating experience was free of painful, distracting winds. And if our costumes called for flimsy tank tops, so be it. I cannot imagine anything more depressing than having to be Darth Vader in a bright pink parka. Or a princess in a navy peacoat.

Plus, because no one was wearing jackets, my friend Maya and I could get a really solid look at the competition. (We'd usually spend the evening in my building or in her building, three blocks away.) As soon as we'd pass through the metal elevator doors, we'd eye the two or three kids already in there and feel obligated to throw out compliments. "Ah. Ha. Totally get it. You look great." All the while thinking, *What a mess. Pacman doesn't wear a Pacman sweatband and carry a Pacman lunchbox. You're just watering down your concept.*

Let me just add that Maya's building had twenty-five floors and each floor had ten apartments. The building policy was that if a door had a small decoration on it, you were allowed to trick-or-treat there. Most everyone participated, so we're talking 250 stops. About ten candy items per stop. That's 2,500 pieces. Just in her building alone.

I know.

When it was warm enough to play outside, and I was old enough to leave the building by myself (if I promised to stray no more than ten steps away in any direction), maybe at age nine or ten, my friends and I liked to play a game we called Sell. This was like selling lemonade at a lemonade stand, but instead of lemonade, it was old random crap from one of our houses: Bat-

teries from the junk drawer, perfume samples from the bathroom, broken dolls, barrettes, books, pencils. I guess it was like a suburban yard sale except that children were in charge and the merchandise wasn't stuff that parents necessarily wanted to give away. And instead of displaying the goods on a card table in a grassy yard, the junk was laid out on an old ripped sheet covering a chunk of dirty concrete. And instead of waiting for customers to drive by, there were tons of people constantly walking back and forth admiring how cute you were.

"Look at this. Bridget, look at these kids. How much is the pen, dear?"

"The pen?" I'd ask. "Maya, check the chart. The pen was recently marked down, actually. And for you, I'll take another ten cents off. And throw in a free piece of loose-leaf paper. So that will be . . . two dollars, please."

"Two dollars?"

"This is a good pen, miss. A Bic."

"I'm sure it is. Bridget, just give them the money. This is precious."

* * *

Some of my greatest childhood memories are of actively helping my mother find cabs amidst chaotic traffic. From an early age, I had a special, innate ability to spot available taxis from blocks away. It was a superpower. Mom would be frantically hailing a cab on the other side of the street, hoping the driver would make a U-turn and choose us over the thousands of other desperate pedestrians, and I'd say, "There! Over there!" and find us an available one around the corner that no one had spotted yet. (As far as I know, when it comes to cars, suburban kids only help their parents out by sitting still and not hitting their brother.)

One of the saddest things to witness in the city is uninformed tourists frantically hailing a taxi whose availability light isn't on. They don't know that there's a *system*. The white, rectangular light on top of the cab goes on when the meter is not being used. I guess they think you are supposed to just wave at every yellow car and hope for the best.

But that light could not be more noticeable to me. Even though it technically means getting in a car with a strange man, to me it has always said, "You will not have to spend the night in the drizzling rain on a curb." Given how difficult it can be to find an available taxi at certain hours—even for talented taxi spotters—if I'm walking across the street to go to the deli and an available cab goes by, I'll always think, *Ugh. I wish I was going somewhere.* I'll be tempted to actually hail the cab just to take advantage of the opportunity.

But the best thing about being a kid in Manhattan was that, all together, the city served as one big, soothing nightlight/white noise machine. Yes, at times I was scared of crime, but once Mom and I were home, tucked away in our seventh-floor apartment, the images and sounds of the "hustle" down below put me at ease. In the suburbs, there is so much silence that if you hear a creak, you have to wonder if it's an ax murderer. In the city, you can't hear creaks. They blend into the music blaring from a boom box, the honking of traffic, and the sound of buses farting out pollution.

Growing up, I found nothing more relaxing than hearing these sounds of the city every night while looking out the window and counting the lit apartment windows surrounding me. All those people had made it back to their base, too. We were one large urban family split up into millions of tiny compartments. Taking out some toy binoculars I had lying around, and peering into some of those compartments to examine my fellow New Yorkers hand-washing *their* clothes, cooking *their* dinner, and wandering from room to room in *their* underwear—that was the best part.

the hippo and the tortoise

I stood with twenty other fourth-grade Manhattanites in single file, waiting to begin an intense stroll into the wilderness. It was going to be my first significant exposure to nature. "So you want to be real careful and stick to the trail here. The leaves can get slippery if you go too far right, where there's a drop. And poison ivy patches are not far from our left!" our leader roared. He was a tan young man whose dirty, mangled fingernails exuded Crocodile Dundeeness. Some of the boys in my class embraced the warning as an exciting challenge, but I thought, *Wait. Hold on. What is this talk of "be careful"?* I'd been under the impression that this fellow absolutely, positively guaranteed safety. I'd heard of poison ivy, but assumed it would be gated off or sealed up in some capacity for our convenience.

We had just arrived on a weeklong class trip to Frost Valley, New York, a large woodsy campground three or four hours from Manhattan. A trained staff worked there year-round, exposing concrete-accustomed bodies to dams, trails, campfires, and ropes courses.

Anxious and already exhausted, I forged ahead through the uneven terrain, convinced I'd trip on a damp stick or low twisted vine. My thin wool socks were getting cold and wet, even through my high-top Reebok sneakers. When I looked to my right and saw a nearby ledge overlooking what seemed like a mile-long drop, I thought about how I could have accidentally meandered over there and slipped. I realized at that moment that no human being, not even a dirty-nailed hiking specialist, could make guarantees when nature was concerned. Even the most benign, happy mountain trails were clearly wrought with unpredictable, life-threatening elements.

When we eventually made it to our final destination, which was a tall, fairly attractive waterfall emitting a misty cloud, we were told to stand back and enjoy the scenery. But how could I appreciate any of the elegant water flow knowing that one of my classmates could get hit in the head with a flying stone at any moment? And that our so-called guide might not be 100 percent capable of preventing such a crisis? I thought, *For this we are risking our lives?* It all came down to the fact that, despite nature's obvious aesthetic glory, fundamentally there was really *no one in charge.*

This, of course, was in direct contrast to "real life" where there were perfectly reliable authorities at every turn to ensure one's well-being: parents, babysitters, teachers, principals, doctors, lawyers, policemen, and presidents.

For a while it was easy to avoid nature because my mother had zero interest in what it had to offer. I have absolutely no memory of my mother against a natural backdrop, although I do recall her running in heels from furry bees in the park. But the following spring, when I was ten years old, it was decided that Maya, Soomee, and I would spend the month of June at sleepaway camp, and camps were unfortunately located in nature.

Maya, Soomee, and I didn't go to the same school, so we liked the idea of spending an intense amount of time together over the summer. We were also open to escaping the city humidity and being independent, but I think it was our parents who really needed the break. They frantically ordered camp marketing materials, which consisted of pamphlets and video-tapes describing activities, food, and board. Most of the camps were too expensive and too glitzy. Camp Timber Bear's video featured an elaborate montage of girls posing in tight Guess jeans to "Safety Dance." Maya, Soomee, and I were sensitive children who needed a noncompetitive, non-cliquey, nonmateri-alistic, nurturing environment, so our mothers eventually found an affordable camp in the Adirondacks called Camp Woodlake for Girls, which claimed to be founded on a Quaker philosophy. My mother interpreted this to mean "happy and safe," so off to Woodlake we went, highly unprepared for the hard-core wildlife awaiting us.

One of my first nights at camp, I woke up at 3 a.m. with an absolutely nonsuppressible urge to pee. Maya, Soomee, and I had been assigned to a small cabin with six New Englanders, and I'd gotten stuck sleeping on a sunken-in top bunk. Al-though I was reluctant to dangle from the rickety metal ladder of my bed in pitch darkness, bladder pressure eventually won out; I cautiously climbed down and walked through the damp, shadowy woods with my dim Garfield flashlight to the "bath-room," which was nearly half a mile away. Once darkness fell, this barely functioning group of port-a-potties turned into a nat-ural cesspool of potentially poisonous bug life. Worse than the assortment of misfit chubby insects with stingers was the alarm-ing number of spiders. Specifically, daddy longlegs.

I was squatting over one of the bowls, desperately trying not to make eye contact with any creatures, when suddenly I saw a black dot floating by my knee. I told myself that it was only a dot—a tiny dust ball adrift on the breeze. But as I performed the double take, I realized the dot was attached to eight or ten barely visible, super-elongated limbs making their way toward my inner thigh. It would have been alarming to have any spider wander into my crotch, but the combination of being deceived by a horny dot while in the vulnerable state of urinating instigated a panic attack and I pulled my shorts up midstream. Before I could catch my breath, I glanced down and saw the lanky beast, which had fallen on the sticky floor. I think it actually gave me the finger. One of its legs slowly turned upward toward the sky.

When I got back to my cabin, still shaken, I tried to be mature and simply go back to sleep, but as I lay in my bunk all I could see were dots. On the ceiling, walls, beds. I didn't know if they were just blameless dots of dirt or shitty conniving dots with hidden agendas. After a few minutes, I woke Gertrude, my crunchy counselor, and asked if I could sleep with her. "Gertrude! There are dots everywhere. Can I sleep with you?"

"Sure," she replied. "I'm naked, though. I sleep naked. Every night. So only if you don't mind that . . ."

I chose freethinking nude counselor over army of deceptive spiders, and spent one of the worst nights of my life lying stiffly under starchy sheets, surrounded by a vast amount of exposed, b-acne covered, patchouli oil–smelling skin.

Even though I haven't seen one in years, daddy longlegs continue to disturb me, mostly on a philosophical level. Because if and when you take off the legs, you just have . . . THE DADDY. This crazy concentrated daddy dot. And what the hell is going on in the daddy dot? The daddy dot tells the legs to move, so if there are no legs, it must be, like, totally freaking out. It must be this intense ball of cerebral frustration. If I ever had the courage to talk to a daddy dot, I'd be like, "Dot, for God's sake, *calm down*. Now you'll be known and liked for who you really are . . . and not just for your long legs."

* * *

In addition to disturbing spiders, Camp Woodlake was filled with outdoor water sports. In between enjoyable arts and crafts, jewelry-making, and jazz dance classes (in which I learned a choreographed kick-ball-change routine to Yaz's "Bad Connection"), campers were required to swim in an ice-cold lake covered by a thick oily film, and laden with all forms of algae-type plant life. There was no way to doggie paddle and not get your foot entangled in a prickly weed that could possibly drag you underwater or keep you from getting back to land in one piece.

But the really unfortunate part was that there was a lot of canoeing on the lake, and canoeing ability was revered at Camp Woodlake, and, to my utter dismay, I was truly gifted at canoeing. Gifted lake canoers were asked by a highly selective canoeing committee to go on frequent overnight canoeing trips involving rapids. *Rapids.* Saying no to the committee was not an option. That would have been like refusing to accept an Olympic medal.

Every few days, I attended these overnight rapid trips, along with one experienced "guide" and five older campers, who actually enjoyed talking "canoe shop." (This included heated arguments over the benefit of a slight wind versus a big gust and discussions about a controversial paddle-cleaning technique involving deodorant.) Since I didn't have the physical strength to be the bow, I served as the stern, which meant that I was the one responsible for navigating the boat between deadly rocks. We were repeatedly told to avoid the ones that were known to spin canoes around and around in their white foam, often killing the passengers. I was expected to reply, "Okay, sure. Totally. No problem. I'll just avoid those rocks then. Yay."

Then, at night, as we gathered around campfires to sing songs from the seventies about the joys of frolicking among trees, we'd be told to please cover every ounce of skin lest a

Lyme tick suck our blood and give us a long-term disease that could permanently screw with our muscles and joints.

Canoeing was so important at Camp Woodlake that they annually celebrated a midsummer holiday called Float Night. During the dinner portion of the evening, at which they served watery mashed potatoes and slabs of what I think was supposed to be beef, the twelve best canoers at camp were presented with wooden paddles that had existed since the beginning of Camp Woodlake time. Each of our names was added to a list of notorious former canoeing stars. Then, for the "performance" part of the evening, the entire camp gathered at the lake by a bonfire to watch the twelve honorees get into canoes and present a well-rehearsed canoe water ballet by swirling around in circles and weaving in and out of lines in perfect unison.

The odd part was that the audience was at the same level of the water, so all anyone saw was the sides of canoes going back and forth. Only a person watching with a bird's-eye view from a plane could appreciate the artistry.

Horseback riding through nature's trails was also big at Camp Woodlake. The first time we were introduced to the animals in the smelly barn, the riding counselors explained how important it was to appear confident when saddling up because horses sense fear the way dolphins hear high-pitched noises. But how could I possibly attempt to ride a horse for the first time knowing that my nervousness was potentially making things even more life-threatening? To safely ride a horse, it seemed, one needed years of acting training. I had taken a couple of drama classes and played charades, but hadn't learned serious performance techniques. Plus, even if I could somehow manage to trick a horse into thinking I was totally calm, the relationship would be built on deception. It was a lose-lose situation, and I refused to ride, thus saving myself from yet another death-defying, nature-related scenario.

I masochistically attended Camp Woodlake again and again with Maya and Soomee because we liked our bunkmates and worshipped Sally, our favorite counselor, who once explained the definition of a hand job by demonstrating on my arm with Lubriderm lotion. But it all came to an end after my fifth summer. When I got home to New York City and started to unpack my trunk, a daddy longlegs slyly crept out of a plastic baggie full of socks and extra iron-on name labels. It had had the audacity to follow me home. I immediately ran screaming and Mom had to smother it with a nearby pack of AA batteries. As I shivered with fear by the bedroom door, I promised myself that I would never again return to Woodlake, and, moreover, would avoid nature at all costs from that day forward.

Because I firmly believe in sticking to these kinds of promises, a decade later, when a group of my college friends decided to take a week off of our first sophomore semester and go camping in a nearby Connecticut forest with tents and all that jazz, I politely declined. I preferred to stay on campus, where life was safe and convenient, and asserted that nature was too unpredictable and that, more important, there was really *no one in charge.*

I would soon regret that decision because the next day, while entering the dining hall, I touched a greasy doorknob, which I'm fairly sure transmitted the germ that led to a sudden crippling flu. By the end of that evening, my temperature had reached 103, and I'm one of those people who never get a legit fever—usually just a 99. In a clogged, sweaty, and panting daze, I lay totally incapacitated on my back, gasping at ghostly hallucinations and completely unable to eat, drink, or even watch *Party of Five.*

Four days later, I finally felt better. Psyched to be able to socialize and see the light of day again, I skipped out the door of my dorm and got hit by a black BMW.

The fratty student driving the car was actually the most traumatized. He was a junior I'd seen around campus, wearing an absurdly oversized red windbreaker and a baseball cap. He stopped, burst out of the car, and started sobbing. At the same time, shock and adrenalin got me up off my side and running down the block. I'd sprinted a good ten meters when an angelic woman who'd apparently seen the whole thing gently tapped my arm. "How can you be running? Are you okay?"

"Oh, I'm totally fine," I replied, grabbing my knee. I had no visible injuries and my jeans weren't even torn. "Yeah, no, totally, I'm fine now. See, I just got over the worst possible flu and this is supposed be a new healthy chapter of life, so obviously I'm fine . . ."

When the ambulance arrived a few minutes later, I kept repeating, "Yeah, no, guys, I'm fine. This is a new healthy chapter of life! HEALTHY CHAPTER!" They ignored my cries and clasped me to a wooden stretcher.

At the hospital, I was wheeled through long narrow hallways, the front metal bars of my cart banging into idle life-support machines, and was eventually left in a cold, dark room. Forty-five minutes later, a doctor arrived, took X-rays, and told me my femur was broken. Initially, I thought, *Yipeee.* My whole life I'd been dying to actually break something. I can't even tell you how many times I'd fallen—like really hard—and barely even gotten a mark. And it's difficult to receive proper sympathy in the case of internal bruising. Without a cast, there is no proof. So to break something meant that when people asked me, "Is it *broken*?" I could finally proudly reply, "Indeed it is."

But when I got home from the hospital, the ramifications of the injury set in. I had throbbing pain on one side of my body and I had to be bathed by my friend and dormmate Katie, on one of those off-white plastic shower stools that my grandmother owns. It was uncomfortably reminiscent of my tub experiences with Aida, my old housekeeper.

Then, two days later, as I lay in my cast eagerly waiting for my friends to return from bonding with Mother Nature, I was sued by J.Crew.

Their legal department started sending me notices claiming that I had ordered forty-five barn jackets and fourteen kiwi tweed cardigans from a canceled checking account.

Turns out the guy responsible was also wanted by the Connecticut police for killing squirrels. And for months, one unorganized, rambling police officer after another filed into my apartment to visit me as I hobbled around on my crutches. Each needing to clarify whether they had come for the car accident or the stealing of conservative clothes.

Now, it's not like I hadn't encountered the chaos of civilization prior to this saga. I wasn't so sheltered that I hadn't heard of or seen far worse things happening to innocent people. There was just something particularly insane about turning down a trip to go camping because nature felt too unsupervised, only to get knocked around by metropolitan living.

And sadly, it has become increasingly apparent that most of the parents, babysitters, teachers, principals, doctors, lawyers, policemen, and presidents I once thought were *in charge* were really just winging it.

The only thing that has truly helped me cope with this real-

ization was the discovery of a recent news story about a baby
male hippo. He was washed ashore after being separated from
his herd by the torrential rains following the tsunami in East
Asia in 2004, and has apparently since become *best friends* with a
130-year-old tortoise. According to the articles, the friendship
may not be completely mutual because the tortoise might simply be "tolerating" the hippo, but they are inseparable. *They take
long walks together.* Experts are completely beside themselves.
Why this isn't on the front page of every newspaper and breaking into already scheduled programs on all the major TV net-
works is beyond me. This strikes me as more newsworthy than
ANYTHING going on right now.

An image of the duo has become my computer screensaver.
The hippo is snuggling up against the tortoise and the tortoise
has the same loving but slightly irritated expression my mom
used to make whenever she found me smoking pot. When I look
at their hilarious bond, an unforeseen result of a startling natural disaster, the pit in my stomach regarding all the inevitable
chaos of life feels a little less incapacitating. For a second I allow
myself to consider that maybe things do happen for a reason.

the traveling monchhichis

"Wendaay, I want to see some exotic flowers and thorns from a safe distance. I saw an ad in the pamphlet about a veery nice trolley tour through the Orlando countryside."

I was seven and Mom and I had been at Disney World for three days. We were purposely avoiding rides like Space Mountain because they appeared unsafe and neither of us could understand why anyone in their right mind would *choose* to be scared. So I didn't object when Mom insisted we take the trolley. It'd be boring, but at least we wouldn't be soaring at lightning speed into darkness, or need to be rescued via helicopter after someone's seatbelt got caught in a wheel causing a massive technical malfunction.

Because my mother doesn't believe in reading maps or signs with arrows, she asked every adult that came our way for directions, all of whom pointed in the same general direction, and eventually we came upon a line of families organized into rows by ten or fifteen yellow cones. Once we finally climbed into our compartment, as I was yawning, thick black padded bars shot down from above, bolting us securely into our seats. One bar clamped our chests, another gripped our waists, and another shackled our shins. Then there was a jolt and we found ourselves going steeply upward in short, quick jerks.

"Uh . . . Mom?"

"Wendaay, remain calm. SOMEONE! HELLO? WHAT IS HAPPENING HERE?! STOP THE RIDE!!!!!"

In her exhaustion, Mom had misread the pamphlet. What we thought was the trolley ride was really Space Mountain's newest competitor, the Great Railroad or something. The ride had not been fully visible from the entrance area and we'd somehow been oblivious to the nearby screams. And in my mother's fervor, it never occurred to her that tons of people *wouldn't* eagerly crowd on line to make a lazy circle around the theme park. No one could hear my mother's hysteria, and it was too late to change course, so we soared downward on our very first and very last rollercoaster ride ever. What followed was a blur of terror, nausea, and wind-induced facial pain.

When the ride came to a close and we pulled into the station, we both looked like Monchhichis, those half human, half chimp-like dolls who sucked their thumbs and whose tufts of hair shot straight up when you shook them senseless. In complete silence, we stumbled back to the hotel and straight to our room to recuperate, with an unspoken understanding that, going forward, we would be extra careful to avoid situations that could in any way, shape, or form be considered remotely even slightly adventurous or adrenalin-pumping.

My mom and I are not the traveling type. We've never felt truly at ease outside our natural habitat of the Upper East Side. But because she wanted me to see other cities and wanted us to be a normal family that took bonding vacations, Mom continued to plan short, relatively manageable annual excursions. Which were still inevitably wrought with roller-coasteresque anxiety.

At the airport, we'd rush through the terminal, waving our arms in unison down the ramp to the gate, despite the multiple hours we had to spare before boarding. But the peak of the frenzy was actually in the *house* hours before, as we prepared our luggage for check-in. We'd spend a good forty-five minutes decorating our suitcases with multicolor sticker dots (at least ten per square foot) so that they'd stand out like freakishly dressed children, and couldn't possibly be mistaken for property owned by a normal person. More important than the dots was displaying our name, phone number, address, and destination in thick black marker on two or three large pieces of paper scattered throughout the clothes inside. The two laminated ID tags attached to the handle and zipper were just not enough.

Our earliest family vacations were to West Palm Beach, Florida, over my spring break, where we'd stay with Grandma Ann, my mom's mom, who lived in one of those old-age villages. Every morning, while Grandma Ann took her quiet time and stayed in the house to read up on the stock market, Mom and I would travel to the pool across the street. Cars, mostly driven by short, fragile old people, rather infrequently chugged past. But because the road seemed dangerously wide compared to streets in the city, and the crosswalk lines were faded, Mom insisted we take a prearranged car service. Across the street. Every morning, in flowered one-piece bathing suits (Mom's with a flowy skirt attached to cover any small bits of cellulite) and tight rubbery blue swimming caps sucked to our heads, we were greeted by a different uniformed driver. Expecting an airport pickup, these men were highly perplexed when we'd scoot in half-naked with towels, suntan lotion, and baggies of fruit.

"Just take us to that pool just over there, please." Mom would say. "Yes, *right there*. Thank you. Here's twenty-five dollars."

Mom and I spent most of our time at the pool suntanning. She was uncharacteristically at ease with excessive sun exposure and never insisted I apply lotion on my face. I loved the way I looked with a pink strip across my upper nose and cheeks. Once I was old enough to wear makeup, I unfortunately felt compelled to simulate that strip every winter with bright pink blush. For years I looked like a drunken old lady at a wedding who had had a severe makeup mishap.

Mainly I liked going to West Palm Beach because Mom and I would get to watch the Oscars—which usually coincided with the vacation—on a big, eighteen-inch TV screen in Grandma Ann's living room. I have a very distinct memory of watching *Out of Africa* win nearly every award, shaking my head, and feeling acutely frustrated that *Splash* wasn't a contender. Daryl Hannah had played a *mermaid*, for heaven's sake. Even though neither of us had ever seen any of the movies nominated, Mom and I enjoyed looking at the outfits and watching the "in memory of" part where they play a montage of movie clips of all the people who've died that year. Mom would make small moans during this segment. "Hmm. Wow, he died. He was one of my favorites back in the day." "Come *on*," I'd whine. "Just someone I know. Not another black-and-white clip."

Eventually Mom felt that suntanning and Oscar-watching in

Florida was limiting, and that it was time to expose me to new and different cultures. Expenses aside, she could not have handled the logistics involved in actually leaving the country, so she found less overwhelming substitutes. Like when I was ten, instead of taking a trip to Mexico, Mom settled on quasi-leaving the country to go to *New* Mexico. After a day of touring Santa Fe, she became obsessed with turquoise jewelry and adobe. At restaurants, she'd marvel at the Aztec quilts on the walls, lean in, and say, "Wendaay, it's like being in a foreign country . . . only . . . we can drink the water!" Unfortunately, both of us spent much of the week debilitated by altitude sickness, and I left the city wearing a bolo tie.

The fact that Amos is actually from Albuquerque gives my mother endless pleasure. Whenever Amos and I travel to visit his mom and sister she'll say, "And they really do live in those adorable clay houses? I just loved those clay houses. Remember those? He's such a good man for you."

Little does she know that Amos is on a major campaign to finally deprogram me from nearly everything I learned to fear under my mother's regime. He has accepted the fact that I'll probably never go rock climbing or downhill skiing or roller-coaster riding, but he doesn't want me limiting myself more than absolutely necessary. He hopes we can at least go ice-skating or even roller-skating or maybe on a simple walk along a flat nature trail every now and then. Because I truly want us to be able to explore the world together in a calm fashion, I'm willing to take baby steps.

Amos's latest lesson took place a couple of months ago after we flew to New York from Albuquerque. He insisted we *very casually* stroll to the baggage claim, and even stop by the restrooms on the way—my mother's worst nightmare.

"But what if someone mistakes my bag for theirs?!" I cried.

"Two words for you," Amos replied. "Sticker dots."

"I know, but it's really easy to mistake bags for one another."

"*Sticker dots,*" he repeated.

"Right. Okay. You're right. I'll be cool. Should we stop for some water?"

Then I remembered that earlier he hadn't let me insert the crucial three sheets of paper with all my contact information inside my suitcase to complement the info on the outer tags. My heart started pounding.

"Forget it, I don't want water. Come on, we've got to get to our bags!"

I felt like we were a set of irresponsible parents who weren't going to make it to school in time to pick up our first grader.

When we finally arrived, there was a small crowd still waiting, but most people were contently rolling their belongings off in carts. My bag was nowhere in sight. Even Amos seemed worried.

Then, suddenly, there was a lone red bra. Just drifting down the conveyor belt.

There was a murmur in the crowd. Everyone was mumbling, "Oh, that's kinda funny."

I thought, *Oh, that's kinda funny . . . wait, that's MINE.*

And one by one, my clothes came shooting down the ramp.

It was impossible not to laugh as we gathered the scattered pieces of my wardrobe together in seven large Continental plastic bags. But I officially calmed down when every item was accounted for, and when I received a cool five hundred dollar voucher from the airline.

Amos's ideas are well-meaning, but if we'd waited much longer I could have ended up with a majorly lackluster wardrobe. As soon as I got home I filled out a dozen contact information sheets for both of us for next time. I think he'll be grateful I did.

leaving the lower math group

For as long as I can remember, my mother has subtly stressed the importance of getting a prestigious education so that I could become (a) a litigator for high-profile class action suits, (b) a corporate businesswoman in charge of mergers, or (c) a dermatologist with a thriving private practice for teens with acne. It wasn't remotely about gaining prestige or excessive material wealth (my mom isn't like that at all), but in her mind attending highly selective schools would enable me to pursue any of these three vocational scenarios, which in turn would guarantee financial stability. ("You can never be dependent on a husband because you might get divorced or he could die. You need to make enough money as a single parent to live comfortably, and to send *your* kids to private school, so that they, too, can support a family as a single parent.")

But early on, even at the age of five or six, I felt anxious when exposed to anything outside my comfort zone that felt too challenging. The mere existence of alphabet blocks made me nervous; minus signs gave me heart palpitations; the map of the United States induced nausea. So even though I was already a perfectionist (I made "to do" lists in my head during naptime: (1) return *The Travels of Babar* to library, (2) talk to Ms. Donovan again about yesterday's addition problem, (3) check kiln for my clay mug to take home, (4) ask Mom for a new, brighter napping mat), I worried I might be incapable of functioning in those types of esoteric professional worlds.

Even benign games of "pretend" made me tense. Every few weeks I would put on my long navy nightgown and a pair of my mother's smaller pumps, and sit at my white wooden desk with my legs crossed, pretending to be someone important at an office. I would shuffle old spelling tests, imagining they were important files for a frustrated client, and take out one of my mother's old checkbooks and sign dozens of voided checks, making the *W* in my signature enormous with a slow, wide hand motion and the rest of my name really, really small and entangled-looking. (From what I'd witnessed in banks and stores and on TV, successful grown-ups had incredibly messy and convoluted signatures.) But as I would talk about the rise and fall of today's economy with Theodore, my stuffed elephant in need of financial assistance, I felt like leaning in and whispering, "Go with another company. I'm full of shit. I'm thinking of getting out of this field." I'd end up complaining to him about the corporate bureaucracy and how the arches of my feet ached from the heels. Then I'd press my temples, squint my eyes, and ask for an Excedrin.

I'd experience a similar frustration when playing dermatologist. At first, it was fun to gather all the medication in the house into a heap at the edge of my bed and organize them by type: creams, pills, sprays, lozenges. And I liked informing make-believe patients about side effects. ("This pill will help your rash but might dry you out. I'd recommend also using this topical ointment.") Like check signing, it was also gratifying to write prescriptions. I had a square, white Hello Kitty pad and was good at fake cursive. Inevitably, though, I'd lose confidence, worry I was giving wrong advice or suggesting an incorrect dosage, and want to refer all my regulars to other specialists.

The only pretend job that felt right was stationery store

owner. I loved the idea of owning a stationery store because I'd been to one nearby that smelled like piney sawdust—the scent of freshly cut paper—and was really well swept. It also had a long, plentiful candy aisle filled with Snickers, a variety of fruity, chewy candies, Life Savers, and gum. The owner seemed to have full access to this assortment as he sat behind the counter all day watching soaps on a tiny TV. Playing stationery store owner at home was simple and fun. I'd arrange lollipops, Now and Laters, and Big League Chew packets on the floor of the living room, sit Indian-style, and stare into the television set, periodically fixing the antennae, nibbling on sugar, and smelling pads of paper. There was no stress involved because I was confident in my stationery-store-owner abilities.

But knowing this occupation did not fit into my mother's formula for financial success, I had a hunch that I was intellectually lacking in some significant way and would probably be unable to support a family as a single parent one day.

This notion was confirmed at the start of second grade when the class got divided into two levels for math and English, and I was placed in the lower groups. These groups were not overtly labeled "lower," but, since my grammar school only had twenty-four kids in each grade, everyone knew who the really disruptive, sloppy, nose-picking kids were (Evan, Nicky, and Dan F.), and it wasn't a coincidence that they were suddenly all in the same math and English classes. I was disappointed to be put in these groups, but I wasn't insulted. On some level I was impressed that the teachers also saw little intellectual potential in me. They were perceptive.

Within weeks, I came to love being in the lower groups. I worked hard, did well, and thought I seemed like one of the smartest not-that-smart kids.

The lower and upper divisions stayed pretty much the same

from then on, although every few years someone would quietly get moved up or down. One day in fifth grade, that someone was me. As I was walking to my homeroom one morning, Mrs. Fenkle, a pudgy math teacher who wore a lot of corduroy, stopped me in the hall and asked me to take a quick stroll with her to the water fountain.

"So, Wendy, we're making some adjustments and we've decided you are going to change math and English classes. You'll start in my class next week."

"What? But, no. I don't belong there. I'm happy where I am," I said, biting off the remaining white portion of my thumbnail.

"You'll be fine. We can work outside of class to get you up to speed if you want. See you then."

As she sped off, it seemed like the friction of her corduroy pants might cause her inner thighs to burst into flames. My eyes filled with tears.

The teachers had foolishly mistaken working hard for being smart.

Within the hour, I developed hives all over my body. When I dropped off a few textbooks in my cubby, my homeroom teacher, a quiet, thin man with a vicious comb-over, noticed the raised red blotches on my face and sent me to the school nurse. This was not a good thing, because if you were feeling remotely out of sorts a visit to the nurse would send you over the edge. Nurse Crowl had long ratty hair and a deep voice that was the opposite of soothing. And she was morbidly obese and usually out of breath. Plus, no matter what the ailment, she would tell you to lie down on a stained Army cot that reeked of mothballs. (My friend Emily once hurt her wrist playing volleyball in PE, and the nurse told her to calm the heck down and take a nap. The next day Emily's mom took her to a real doctor and discovered she'd chipped a bone.) On this particular day, another kid with a bloody nose was already lounging, so she told me to "take it easy" and handed me some Tylenol.

"This will help the itchiness?" I asked, scratching my chin with the Velcro on my Trapper Keeper.

"Yes."

"It's really bad, though. Maybe I should take extra strength?" (To this day I have never understood why anyone would buy or give out regular strength anything. Even if you have a mild ache, why not just take extra strength and be thorough about it?)

"I don't have many extras left. Regular will do." Not only did she give me the wrongest medication ever, but she was also stingy with it.

Despite being placed on numerous allergy medications, I ended up having hives for my entire first year in the advanced classes, hyperventilating my way through decimals that went past the tenth place and spelling tests with too many silent *b*'s, like in *comb*. From the moment I arrived home from school at 4 p.m., I would frantically study for hours, stroking the welts on my body with a soft, thick brush. When I wasn't studying, all I could think about was how calm and itch-free life would be if I didn't have to worry about academics. I'd see an elderly person dragging their arthritic bones across the street and think, *I'd do anything to be an old person. They have it so good. They don't have to feel challenged by long division in an upper math group.*

It was just incredibly important that I not allow the higher expectations of the upper classes to keep me from getting an A on every test and paper. I *had* to get straight As, so that I might still have a shot at becoming a successful single parent one day.

But once I achieved all As, I figured it was because of my relentless effort as opposed to being an inherently smart person.

Tracking in schools is so fucked up. I mean, it didn't just affect the way I thought about myself. To this day, I still think of other people according to how they were categorized back then, too. Recently my mom ran into this guy Jack's mom, who told her that Jack is now a second-year surgical resident in Boston. My gut reaction was, "A doctor? Really. That's rather surprising. He was in the lower math group."

My lack of intellectual confidence was further compounded by the incessant, over-the-top flattery I received from my grandparents, and the accompanying qualifiers offered by my mother. If I showed my grandparents a short story I'd written, like the one called "As My Stomach Turns" (about the behind-the-scenes social dynamics of a greasy hamburger joint), they'd beam, "Wendy, you have a gifted way with words. This was surely THE BEST in the class. You could win a Pulitzer Prize someday." My mother, fearing I'd get a swelled head, would add, "Well, all the kids' stories were good. It's cute, Wen." If I leapt into the air with my feet pointing upward and my arms flailing in all directions, my grandparents would beam, "Wendy, you have something special. You bend perfectly. You could be the best gymnast in the entire world!" My mother would respond, "You look great, Wen. But guys, really, all the girls are graceful like that. Two of the kids in her grade just got into a professional production of *The Nutcracker*." If I told my grandparents that I was going to a birthday party the next weekend, they'd say, "Wendy, we are blown away. You are so popular. You have a unique, special ability to connect with people." As if on cue, Mom would counter, "Everyone is friends with everyone these days. Her class is a close-knit group." Because they were constantly wildly impressed by the most basic of skills, my grandparents slowly lost all credibility. I thought, *Since I clearly can't trust a single thing they say, maybe I suck at everything.*

My mother later admitted to me that she was actively worried I'd become a cocky bitch if she didn't add qualifiers to my grandparents' praise. But as a psychologist, she should have known that their suspiciously excessive compliments (probably combined with her dismissal of them) only made me more insecure.

Over the next few grade school years, when my teachers began to assign scary research assignments, I made sure to pick topics that were as obscure as possible. I wasn't a slacker, I was just easily overwhelmed by too much information and figured I'd have a better chance of getting the A I needed if resources were limited and expectations were lowered. Like once, in fifth grade, we had to get into groups of three and do a research paper on an important scientific issue affecting society. Most students picked exciting topics like "earthquakes" and "the diminishing ozone." I got together with Emily and our friend Tracy and persuaded them to investigate "the solid waste disposal crisis in New York." Not involving feces and toilets, thank God, just general garbage. Although it would not be glamorous, for me it was the calmest way to go—there would probably be less textbook information out there on the waste disposal crisis because it was relatively under the radar. I knew this because my second cousin, Eddie, was a city engineer, and he had recently cornered me at a wedding reception on Long Island to explain a secret, growing concern about landfills and "how the mayor didn't know where to put people's crap."

Since presentations seemed less frightening to me than research papers, I convinced our teacher that, given the subject matter, it was more appropriate for my group to prepare a multimedia lecture. I explained that we could even use my grandfather's video camera to do simple man-on-the-street interviews. It would be an exposé!

With my grandfather following two steps behind, we spent

the following weekend walking around the Upper East Side, ordering him to take powerful footage of beeping garbage trucks and smelly trash cans. We took turns yelling valuable garbage information into the camera over loud background drilling and traffic noise. "BEHIND ME IS SOME OF THE GARBAGE FROM NEW YORK. LOOK AT IT CAREFULLY. WALK WITH ME. IT EVENTUALLY GETS TAKEN TO A BIG . . . AREA SOMEWHERE. THAT'S RIGHT, THIS GARBAGE THAT YOU SEE BEHIND ME GETS PUT IN A PLACE WITH OTHER GARBAGE. IN A BIG PLACE SOMEWHERE. NOW LET'S GO TO EMILY. HERE'S EMILY—Emily, stand over there. Okay, go . . ." Then we talked to the people of New York City with a fake microphone to get *their* perspective. We wandered up to frantic strangers exiting the subway and asked the thought-provoking question, "How do you feel about the solid waste disposal crisis in New York?"

Our field reporting busted the issue right open. Most people said things like, "Well, I didn't know there was a crisis. But if there is one, I certainly think it's bad." Ultimately, we proved two significant things: (1) no one knew about the crisis, and (2) everyone thought a crisis was a negative thing.

One inquisitive man asked, "What *is* the crisis?" Tracy mumbled something about a technical malfunction and we scurried away. We had no idea what the actual crisis was. We were not prepared for such pressing questions. But once the video bits were combined with a few pie charts, we performed a profoundly pointless lecture in front of our peers and somehow got an A minus.

By the time I reached eighth grade, my grades were very good and it seemed like I was securely on my way to becoming a confident lawyer, dermatologist, or businesswoman. Accordingly, like all the kids in the upper classes, I applied to the five private high schools in the city with the best college acceptance records.

Getting into these selective high schools was a major to-do. I had to ask for two recommendations (one from a teacher and one from an "unbiased" nonrelated adult who knew me well), send in writing samples, and go on endless rounds of anxiety-provoking interviews, which I've since blocked out. Mom had to write numerous essays about why I was a better candidate than other children. She stayed relatively composed during this process, though, because she had gone through it before when I had applied to nursery school.

Apparently, it's harder to get your infant into New York City nursery programs than it is to get into most Ivy League colleges. My mother told me that during one of my first nursery school interviews, when the condescending woman asked me my age, I began to cry. Mom gulped and thought we'd blown it. But then, while heaving hysterically, I managed to hold up three fingers, thus answering the question both promptly and accurately.

I got my nursery acceptance letter the next week, but it might have been Mom's essays that did the trick. She had submitted pages of prose to each school, convincing the strict admissions committees that I was the perfect toddler with a blindingly bright future. I recently found one of these essays. This is an excerpt of what she wrote (verbatim):

"At each stage of growth a new facet of her remarkable growing self-hood emerges. Yet, at 4½ she also seems to possess a quality I observed since babyhood—a strong sense of knowing what she wants."

All I really wanted was to avoid scary academic challenges and own a stationery store.

And despite the fact that I no longer broke out in hives on a regular basis, I still felt this way when I was admitted to a small, private high school on the Upper West Side. A strict, Episcopalian, all-boys institution that had turned coed in the early eighties, it prided itself on its intensive old-school curriculum.

When I walked to the mailbox in front of my building to send in my deposit and registration letter, I lifted the perfectly pine-scented envelope to my nose, sniffed, and sighed. With four years of high school, four years of college, and sixty or so years of law, business, or dermatology looming ahead, I suspected this would be my last chance to calmly soak up the glorious goodness of a well-made piece of paper.

the pull of lycra

"Wendy. You are not wandering into the night and getting into a cab with a strange driver looking like some kind of . . . I don't know . . . porn actress!" My mother was taking a break from gnawing on a Cornish game hen wing to scream at me.

"Everyone dresses like this," I roared back. "It's no big deal! No one even notices."

I adjusted the underwire of my bra.

"Change right now, Wendy! You're going to freeze!"

"MOTHER. This is what I'm wearing."

"You cannot look like that out in this city!"

My mother had no problem with me looking slutty. She was all for embracing my newfound high school sexuality. It was really just an issue of safety on the city streets. Had I been wearing the same thing on a date with a nice boy, I would have encountered no resistance whatsoever.

Like many of the girls in my ninth-grade class, I had recently become less interested in what was *on* my shirts—a cute *Far Side* cartoon, a shiny bolt of lightning, a sweet embroidered pocket—and more interested in how big my boobs looked *in* them. The innocent cotton and polyester blends of eighth grade were quickly being replaced with stretchy materials. On this chilly

November night—the night before Thanksgiving—I had dressed strategically for my very first *real* high school party, which I hoped would be like the one depicted in *Say Anything*—couples making out in the closet, drunken girls playing guitars and singing about their ex-boyfriends, boys complimenting your outfit or marveling at your curves from afar. I hadn't yet met the High School Boyfriend, and in order to get as much male attention as possible, I was wearing a white, Lycra, boat-neck shirt, a thin bra that caused a nipple hard-on, and a short, tight, tubelike black skirt that could also be used as a headband. I had bought the skirt at Units, a store on Madison Avenue that mass-produced colored chunks of elastic and labeled them clothes. I was also wearing black platform clogs. They had come with thick black bands that would keep the back of your heels in place, but I'd cut those off in hopes of looking less clean cut. My hair was brown, down to my shoulders, and flipped all the way to the right side in a messy tangle.

I guess I did look a little like a porn actress. I say this only because one Saturday the following spring, when I was wearing a similar outfit while lounging in Central Park with some friends, some dude surreptitiously filmed me eating yogurt off the back of a spoon. Two weeks later I was seen making licking gestures in slow motion on a public access porn show called "Betsy's House of Young Lust." Really. Two of my friends saw it—independently—while channel surfing. I was outraged that I'd been objectified in such a manner, but didn't feel like going through the trouble of trying to do something about it, so I never told my mother. And, to be perfectly honest, I was too entertained by the randomness of the incident to let it affect my fashion choices—which I also hoped would make me more popular.

My high school's formal dress code (no sneakers, no jeans, no T-shirts), designed to keep kids focused on their studies, definitely added to the pressure to conform. As a girl, in order to be cool, you had to wear pearls (real or fake) and one of those headband skirts. It was also preferable to have long, silky blond or brunette hair you could flip back and forth in front of your face with a provocative hand gesture. None of the girls could see out of both eyes at the same time. I tried to grow my hair long and do the flip, but never quite nailed it. Strands of my hair floated up and around in various directions in what appeared to be a perpetual cloud of static.

I did feel lucky to go to this school, but sometimes it really seemed like *Beverly Hills 90210* (*New York City 10023*) contained in one windowless, red brick building. (Apparently, when they built the school in 1905 or something, the numerous shootings in the area made exposed glass a hazard.) The long entrance hallway was lined with wool-covered couches, and every morning, senior jocks wearing varsity jackets would sit with their legs hanging off the armrests and rate the girls as they walked by, yelling out scores from one to ten. Occasionally, in the midst of this, some celebrity like Ivana Trump or Jane Pauley would stroll by to attend a parent-teacher conference. A number of students were children of celebrities and many of them lived in huge apartments and had parties every weekend while their parents were away at country houses.

Such was the case on this night, when I had so carefully dressed in fashionably risqué attire for a party at my classmate Hillary's house on Central Park West.

"Wendy . . ." My mother continued to nag. (Not "Wendaay" this time. My mother doesn't drag out my name when she's angry.) "At least wrap a cardigan or something around your waist. And wear a long coat. And remember, call the car service when it's time to come home. Or share a cab. You are NOT to get into a cab by yourself at a late hour. And you are to call me before you leave. Hillary's house has a doorman, *right*?" Going out at night to an apartment building without a doorman was not an option.

"Yes."

"It is, what, eight o'clock now, and you need to be home by eleven at the *latest*. We need to get up early tomorrow to pick up a pumpkin pie at the gourmet store before getting on the train to Aunt Cynthia's."

"Okay!"

After Mom forced me to cover my bottom half, she handed me two twenty-dollar bills to cover travel expenses. (Forty bucks was far more than I needed, but it was important to her that I have extra cash on me. She always says that if you get mugged, handing over a lot of cash might lessen the risk of physical harm.)

I shuffled into the hall, my feet flopping up and down against the unsupportive soles of my modified shoes.

As I waited for the elevator, Mom stood with the door open, repeating, "Eleven p.m., right? Remember to call, dear, please. Eleven p.m.?"

For years, *I* had been the one nagging incessantly in the hall-way about *her* evening arrival time, sitting with the phone in my lap and waiting for *her* to call before coming home, and anxiously anticipating the sounds of *her* keys after Saturday night dates out on the town. The whole scene felt a little *Freaky Friday*.

In the elevator, I fought my urge to light up the heat-sensitive buttons with hot air from my mouth and maturely tapped the *L* with my index finger. Then I walked as fast as possible down the long hall of the lobby, trying to avoid eye contact with the same night doorman who used to offer me saltines as I paced in my Garfield nightgown, awaiting my mother's return. I didn't want him to see me trying so hard to be a sophisticated teenager. But as I entered the main doorway area, it was impossible not to exchange grins. It was as if we were acknowledging that things would never be the same between us. He put on the taxi light—a small bulb outside the entrance to the building—and a cab came shooting into the driveway. As he opened the door for me, I could see that he was averting his eyes, perhaps not wanting to see me in this new, tainted light.

I got inside, leaned back into the broken spring of the leather seat, and took a deep breath. A part of me wanted to go back home and crawl into my mother's pull-out couch. With every passing block I could feel the umbilical cord being stretched, and this was simultaneously exhilarating and worrisome.

I arrived at Hillary's high-rise building, and went inside to find my best friend, Lucy. Lucy and I had met during the first week of English when a girl named Pam read aloud her essay on the importance of siblings, and then proudly presented the class with a Tupperware bin containing her younger brother's snot. From across the classroom I could see Lucy heaving with laughter behind her long red hair and knew we'd probably be friends for life.

As I walked into the lobby, I saw that Lucy was already milling about with ten or fifteen of our peers. Everyone was in their expected uniforms. To her right were boys in down jackets, Gap jeans, rugby shirts, or bajas (those pullover, hooded, bohemian-like sweater thingies), and Samba sneakers. They smelled of Drakkar Noir. (Intellectually, I've always labeled this scent as "sleazy," and yet it contains some kind of intense pheromone that continues to attract me.) To her left were girls in hoop earrings, long black coats, V-neck sweaters, and headband skirts. They smelled of Ralph Lauren Safari. Some were slumped on the leather couches; others were reapplying a trendy, brown Maybelline lipstick called Toast of New York.

Everyone was waiting to be ushered upstairs by Hillary's doorman. As he approached our group, I saw that an elaborate image of a polo match had been engraved into each one of his tiny cufflinks. Sweat glistened by his sideburns as he attempted to recite an overwhelming number of first and last names, one by one, into the house phone for Hillary's approval. Hillary wasn't being exclusive—she was a popular classmate who was nice to everyone—she just wanted to prevent an excessive number of strangers from attending, and had told the doorman to be abnormally strict in order to keep the bash from getting out of control.

Hillary's building had one of those elevators with an elevator man who would pull an antique lever to carry tenants and guests up and down for ten hours a day. Her family owned two apartments on the twentieth floor, and they had knocked down the separating walls, creating an endless number of guestrooms for famous visiting aristocrats. (Her parents were big political figures.) They kept the door to their house open at all times, and visitors would come and go throughout the week. Rumor had it that if you were doing errands on the Upper West Side and needed a restroom and a quick snack, the family was totally cool with you walking into her lobby, uttering "Hillary" to the doorman, taking the elevator to the twentieth floor, and waltzing into her kitchen for a small cherry tart or stuffed spinach pastry. *If* they were home, Hillary's parents would barely notice anyway—they'd be busy entertaining a diplomat from Italy by the fireplace, or they'd be passed out on one of the recliners, with martini glasses balanced on their chests. Over the course of the next three years, with our high school just around the corner from her building, my friends and I dropped by at least twice a week.

The circa 1920s elevator could only hold the weight of five or six people at once, and Lucy and I waited for the second round so we'd have more time to primp in the lobby mirror before making a grand entrance. Staring discreetly at my reflection, I smoothed out the creases in my headband skirt, folded the waist over, and shifted the material upward, thus raising the length about half an inch. (The real genius of the headband skirt was that the length could be adjusted at any time, so I could easily make it shorter after leaving the house.)

Once inside Hillary's elevator, the density of cologne and perfume was suffocating. The elevator man was fiddling around in his pocket—perhaps looking for an inhaler. I couldn't help but see myself from his perspective, just another rich city kid off to get drunk on someone's parent's champagne. I looked away and sighed, but longed to lean over and clarify, "I'm not really like that. I'm not one of *them*."

The living room area was already crowded with close to seventy ninth graders, mostly from my school, but a few friends of friends who had heard about the shindig by word of mouth. I held Lucy's hand as she weaved through the tightly packed mass of pulsing adolescence toward the master bedroom, where coats were being thrown on a king-size canopy bed.

It was there that a group of twenty freshmen were oh-so-casually doing shots of Scotch while sitting on the varnished hardwood floor. *Yeah, we're doing shots. Just like we've done since we were five. No biggie.*

Then Hillary's dad rushed by to retrieve his wife's pocket-book.

"Have fun kids! We're off to the country!"

Josh, a friendly, beefy lacrosse player whispered, "Jesus. Hillary's parents are soooo cool. Can you imagine having parents that cool? Fucking-A."

I couldn't help but think that her parents were being awfully irresponsible. I've always thought that a parent-type parent was preferable to a friend-type parent. I had plenty of friends and only one parent. I thought, *Thank goodness my mother isn't that cool.*

"Wendy! Lucy! Have a fucking drink!" Josh shouted.

"Nah," I mumbled. Dressing a bit slutty was one thing, but I definitely wasn't ready for drinking. Although I was curious about the whole "getting drunk" process, I was too afraid to participate myself. In grammar school we had been taught that experimenting with drugs or alcohol could easily lead to serious substance abuse or addiction, and I could *not* end up like one of those visiting speakers who talked of insect hallucinations during acid trips. I could barely get a grip on my OCD.

(I've actually only drank alcohol once—in my entire life. Two years after this party, during my junior year, in that very same room of Hillary's house, at her annual New Year's party, I finally decided that being drunk and carefree like my classmates was worth a risk. In an effort to hurry the process along, I ended up guzzling an entire bottle of Scotch on an empty stomach. Digestion has been somewhat problematic ever since.)

Lucy leaned against a bedpost in Hillary's parents' bedroom, took a sip from a shot glass, and contorted her face in disgust. Tim handed her a peach wine cooler. "Here, this will be easier. You can barely taste the alcohol. Trust me. I've done everything."

I sat down with my legs tucked to the right and my thighs tightly pressed together. The goal was too appear as seductive as possible, without showing my underwear. With my left hand pressed into the floor, propping me up, and my right hand massaging my calves in order to keep them from getting pins and needles, I thought, *How the fuck are you supposed to sit in these skirts?* And, *Does Josh think I'm hot?*

Nursing her wine cooler, Lucy sat down next to me and we

listened to the group as they became increasingly inebriated. The girls kept collapsing into fits of laughter because Sally Greer was simply too dizzy to touch her tongue to the tip of her nose. Then this normally demure girl named Robin started blabbing incoherently about how she had such a tight gymnast's body. I felt like I hadn't gotten the memo explaining why sitting uncomfortably on the floor in a crowded circle laughing about pointless things and listening to people brag was supposed to be fun. Hanging out with my stuffed animals was far more enjoyable.

And then, without warning, from another room we heard, "GUYS! THIS IS SERIOUS! SOMEONE JUST THREW UP!"

Mass commotion.

Girls went rushing toward the bathroom in the back of the kitchen where all the madness was apparently going down.

Frightening questions and phrases were circulating the room. "Did you hear? Someone threw up." "How much did she drink?" "Should we call 911?" "She could have alcohol poisoning!" "Remember to roll her on her side. She could choke on her own vomit!"

OH MY GOD. Someone was throwing up *from alcohol*. I felt like I was in one of the bad, grainy educational videos we had seen on substance abuse. Would we all be arrested? Would she die? Had I witnessed too much too soon? Would I never be the same again? Was all innocence lost forever? What would my mother say?

After a mere five minutes, once we heard that Meredith had finished upchucking Chinese takeout and wandered into the living room to eat a chocolate-covered strawberry, we were able to resume normal breathing. The group of panicked children quickly transformed back to a group of savvy drinking experts, as though nothing had happened.

"So what are you guys doing for Thanksgiving?" a slightly bearded guy who I'd never seen before asked, chugging a beer.

"I fucking have to get up early to see the parade with my dad and sister. He's fucking making me," Josh groaned. He was referring to the Macy's Thanksgiving Day Parade.

"What a nightmare," Hillary agreed, digging her perfect teeth into a slice of lime.

Lucy turned to me and whispered, "Wendy, have you ever seen the parade balloons being blown up the night before the parade? On the street?"

"Um. NOOO." Why hadn't I heard about this?

"Where did you think they blew them up? They line the huge balloons along Central Park West and blow them up with machines all night long. People go and watch."

"Wait. They are lying on the *actual* streets? AS WE SPEAK?"

"You wanna go?"

We had only been at the party for a total of twenty-five minutes, but without hesitation we adjusted our headband skirts, fished our coats out from under the pile, said quick good-byes, and hurried out of the building. We hailed a cab and headed straight to Eighty-first Street, where families, couples, and pets were strolling alongside the massive limbs of the beloved stuffed animal–like creatures that hover over the city skyline every year.

For an hour we sat on a curb sipping hot chocolate and marveling at the perfection of Garfield's slowly inflating nose, which took up nearly half of Seventy-ninth Street. I might have looked like a porn actress, but, at that moment, I was right where I belonged.

molly ringwald or ally sheedy?

"Tonight you'll need to drink a lot of water, then fill the cup up at least halfway so we have enough of a sample. Be sure to seal it tightly and write your name on the side label," Mrs. Wilson, my ninth-grade biology teacher, told the class. She was insisting we conduct a urine experiment in which we'd analyze our own liquid waste in all sorts of minuscule ways (pH, vitamin content, dilution). We were to return the next day with a small jar filled with our own pee.

The next morning, while everyone was cringing in shame, trying to cover their samples on the counter by arranging textbooks as protective barriers, I was in a panic. Not because I was embarrassed to show the faint yellow shade of my urine to fellow classmates, but because I was plagued by fear of the equipment, and my lab partner, Marcus, stood next to me seeming equally alarmed. Marcus resembled a daddy longlegs. He was a very thin, quiet boy with a big round head, and he rushed everywhere in spurts, while staying incredibly close to the wall.

Thankfully, however, just as I felt the beginnings of itchy red welts emerging on my face, fate intervened: as Marcus reached for a test tube, he knocked over his pee. It spilled all over my arm and purple, V-neck cotton sweater. I jumped back and he mumbled "Uh, sorry" and awkwardly tried to dab my right boob with a paper towel. After I rushed off to do a full antiseptic scrub and retrieve a gym T-shirt from my locker, I returned to an empty lab station. Because the pee needed to be one day old, Daddy Longlegs had been given another assignment altogether, and I was told to join another group consisting of two total scientific geniuses. Not only did they show me how to finish the experiment and let me copy their write-ups, but they filled me in on the gossip I'd missed: sperm had been found in a slutty girl's specimen.

My lack of intellectual confidence—combined with the pressure to someday make enough money to be able to send my future kids to private school in the event that I should become a single parent—often made the academic demands of high school seem insurmountable. After the urine experiment, I made sure to get lab partners who felt secure in their abilities with Bunsen burners, microscopes, and dissection kits. I would sit on a stool by their side and offer services, like a nurse attending to a surgeon during a heart transplant. "Here's a paper cup full of water—maybe you're thirsty? I know! While you measure out 4.753 mm of hydrogen peroxide and swoosh it around in that potentially explosive glass beaker, why don't I fetch paper towels from the ladies' room in case you need sweat wiped from your brow?"

I tried to reduce my angst in other subjects by staying away from honors classes, avoiding any extracurricular activities that might take time away from studying, and buying hundreds of Cliffs Notes. Even though I read every assigned book meticulously, with a pen in hand, I clung to Cliffs' learning supplements because I got so worried about not understanding the text that I'd end up not having the remotest idea what the hell was going on. Thomas Hardy's *Tess of the d'Urbervilles* sent me into a tailspin of confusion and Joseph Conrad's *Heart of Darkness* was the worst of the worst. Even when I went back to review what I'd read, I found myself at the bottom of a page seeing, "Marlow began again" and thinking, "Wait. Marlow? He's the main guy, right? And what is he beginning?" My anxious mind had wandered and I'd been unconsciously sniffing the potent papery scent of the pages.

During the most stressful moments of reading assignments, when I couldn't find the right Cliffs Notes, I'd bite my cuticles and frenetically rub my teeth against the side of my mouth and munch on inner-cheek skin. At home, witnessing my distress, my mother would do anything to calm me down, from writing my book report summaries with me when she got home from work at 10 p.m., to demanding I watch more sitcoms. She even covered the house with pale-yellow Post-its that read "I love you. You are the best. Worry less." She never dared put direct pressure on me, but as senior year approached, I knew it was important to her that I get into a very prestigious college because it would lead to a very prestigious job that would make me financially independent and where, as a bonus, I'd probably meet a prestigious man to marry (even though he might die or divorce me).

Going to a college that was considered hard to get into was equally, if not more important to my high school's board of directors, because the school needed to maintain an impressive college acceptance ranking. It was also important to the team of freelance college application consultants whom many of the parents hired to help in the strategic planning, and to the in-house college-acceptance advisor, Mrs. Sherplew, who looked and acted like a dehydrated rhinoceros. Each of her nostrils flared and came to an abrupt point, and her college-acceptance lingo came out in a hoarse manner, the result of decades of chain-smoking. "And kids, you are not, I repeat, are *not*, to use the Common Application, oookay? That is acceptance suicide."

Mrs. Sherplew's presence was also stress inducing because rumor had it she was a total wheeler and dealer. If you made her top-ten list of random favorites (there were about a hundred kids in a senior class), she'd make sure to milk her connections and reserve you a spot even before you had finished your second round of private SAT tutoring sessions. Once, my friend Leslie overheard her on the phone saying, "Look, I know she'll never get over a 1300, but if you admit Jen, I'll convince Jonathan to turn down Dartmouth for U Penn." It seemed she not-so-secretly traded students like stocks.

In between trades, Mrs. Sherplew taught a mandatory course to seniors about the college application process. During one of her first few lectures, she led us into a dark classroom and explained that choosing the right college demanded a lot of introspection. I thought we were going to have to do some horrific college-acceptance relaxation chanting exercise, but instead, the opening credits of the terrific movie classic *The Breakfast Club* started playing on a projector. With the volume lowered, she said, "You may have already seen this film, but watch it again thinking specifically about colleges. Which character do you most relate to? Are you an athlete? A princess? A quiet introspective artist? If you are a sporty type, you'll want to focus on going to a jock school with a lot of fraternities. Like Duke or Colby or maybe even Tufts. There are schools that correspond to each type of person . . . we'll go over these more specifically later. First, stereotype yourself."

According to Mrs. Sherplew, it was also imperative that you choose a specific angle for your application essay to make yourself as marketable as possible. Since most colleges longed for diversity, your chances of getting in were higher if you stood out and discussed something oppressive or really, really deep. Were you a minority? If so, hopefully you've experienced some form of prejudice that you could write about. If not, maybe one of your siblings has a learning disability and you think you might want to dedicate your life to brain research. Or even better, maybe you came down with Tourette's and still managed to stay in the popular group. Find a distinguishing detail and run with it!

I thought, *Thank goodness my father died when I was a baby. Phew.*

My mother and I spent weeks brainstorming about how to capitalize on the no-father thing. Eventually she came up with a winning premise that made me seem both mature and politically aware. Dan Quayle had just formally denounced the TV show *Murphy Brown* for insulting American family values, by having the main character choose to have a baby on her own, without a father. I had heard about the ridiculous Quayle incident through word of mouth, but had been too anxious to ever really sit down and watch potentially confusing political news shows. My mother, however, had entrenched herself in the coverage and was delighted to have an opportunity to write about it. As she milked our single-parent status and expressed how the vice president's speech had offended our happy home, I made sure to sit by her side and look up words in a large thesaurus. I had purchased it at the old corner stationery store years before, and its wrinkly, dusty pages were torturously divine.

The most surreal part of the whole college application mania was sitting in the main lobby area of the school during the period when everyone was hearing back and watching peers go totally loony after calling home on the pay phone and having their housekeepers check the mail for any thick envelopes. As soon as a student would find out about an acceptance, word would spread like a gossip forest fire all the way down the long hall and even around the bend to the Swamp, a dark area full of lockers where strange kids practiced witchcraft. Some students would inevitably start to cry. "Why haven't I heard yet? She probably took my spot!" (We were told that most colleges could not take too many kids from one New York City school.) Or, "He got in and not me? He is so dumb! I heard his mother's friend got Norman Mailer to write him a recommendation."

I was able to remain calm during the madness, however, because I had applied "early decision" and gotten in months earlier. I was thankfully all set to go to Wesleyan, a respectable liberal arts university in Connecticut that was known by my peers for having naked student protests. (Essentially, after being forced to watch *The Breakfast Club* for the eighteenth time, I had concluded that while I had many high-maintenance Molly Ringwaldish qualities, I was 75 percent a more radical, somewhat freakish Ally Sheedy.)

All I could do was hope that the strong academic curriculum Wesleyan advertised would help mold me into a more academically confident on-her-way-to-becoming-a-thriving-financially-stable-single-parent-one-day type of person. Or that the abundance of drugs on campus would distract me from worrying too much about it.

neopragmatic hegemonic paradigms

As it turned out, experimenting with drugs was one of my first collegiate experiences with deductive reasoning.

My freshman year at Wesleyan, I lived in a four-person suite, in a central "party dorm," whose coed bathrooms were permanently flooded with bong water. When I was first offered marijuana, I worried that it would hurt my sensitive stomach or that I'd become a spontaneous junkie. The health teachers from grammar school had said that any drug, even pot, could be laced with PCP and cause you to jump out of a large window at any moment. But as I sat on the floor of my cluttered room and hesitantly took my first puff, I thought, *Okay, wait, do I want to jump out of a window? No. Do I want to jump now? No. Now?* In fact, I wanted to giggle, eat candy, and touch suede. Within seconds, the antidrug speakers lost credibility, and I made it my mission to become stoned as often as possible.

The widespread availability of reefer was only a small part of Wesleyan's liberal vibe. I remember taking great pleasure in watching prospective parents who were touring the quaint New England campus stop to read things like "FUCK YOUR SEX" written in huge letters in blue chalk on the sidewalk in front of the admissions building. Instead of the headband skirt that had seemed mandatory in high school, college fashion demanded a piercing or two (eyebrow was ideal), and for a short period many students sported an alternative Amish look with platform shoes, long black cloaks, and white bonnets. I never went Amish, but I did get a belly button ring, which kept me from bending over for a good five months.

I knew my mother and grandparents had worked long hours to save up money so I could have an incredibly privileged education, but sadly that didn't give me the courage necessary to embrace academic challenges by the time college rolled around. I did everything in my power to steer clear of subjects that freaked the crap out of me, like economics or political science or chemistry.

At the very beginning of freshman year, I decided to major in psychology, a field of study that felt familiar because of my mother's career in social work and sex therapy. I also started filling as many core requirements as possible with Wesleyan's "gut" (known for being easy) classes. I couldn't get into the most popular one, Experimental Music, because it was full, but my suitemate Alisa took it, and for her final project she was asked to produce a unique piercing sound with a familiar household object. Despite her petite frame, she ended up dragging an extremely heavy, broken kitchen chair across the classroom floor and getting a thunderous round of applause and an A minus. Although I missed out on this opportunity, I did get into another popular course called The Universe (astronomy for the nonscience person), which actually turned out to be supercomplex. For months I was left contemplating how time and space could possibly be intertwined, and how on earth Stephen Hawking had an extramarital affair with his nurse. Did you know that the scientist eventually left his wife and took off with the sultry caregiver?

Over the course of the next few years, I signed up for numerous "why society is bad" classes, where all we really had to do was rip pictures of women out of magazines, talk to the class about how their emaciated arms were sending the wrong messages to female teens, and mention phrases like "neopragmatic hegemonic paradigms" or the "phenomenology of modernity" or "politically efficacious phantasm." In one of these classes—The Something Demystification of Oppression—we took turns reading aloud passages from *The Color Purple* every week, for four solid weeks, and then watched the movie. As a final assignment, we could either write a thirty-page paper about racism, sexism, and/or homophobia, OR do a final "project." The latter could be anything from an interpretive series of body poses to a thoughtful hum—as long as it evoked sympathy for the exploited. As her final project, one of my more innovative classmates slowly walked to the center of the room, built a dome out of chunks of wax, started a blazing fire at the top, and then extinguished the flames with Evian and tears pouring from her eyes. I never figured out what it meant. For my project, I made a papier-mâché ball, and painted it yellow and green. It symbolized sexual harassment in the workplace.

I also racked up credits by taking an overabundance of beginner dance classes. My junior year African Dance class turned out to be one of the best things ever to happen to me. Every week, we were taught the most erotic moves, including ferocious thrusting of the bust and pelvic areas, to the powerful sounds of live drumming. (The Ghanaian teacher didn't believe in stretching, though, and at least two kids had to sit out every week because of groin injuries.) At the end of the term, once I had recovered from a mild sprain in my lower spine, I was asked to be one of ten dancers in an exquisite recital. I got to twist suggestively while waving a light wooden sword and wearing a sexy green satin sari/straightjacket that ran under my crotch, twice around my thigh, around my waist, across one shoulder, over the left side of my rib cage, and under my armpit.

Shortly after this performance, when my body ached and I could dance no more, I discovered a lot of interesting courses about deafness. Wesleyan has a strong deaf culture, even though, to my knowledge, no one attending the school at that time was actually hearing-impaired. The students who were most passionate about deaf culture could live at Sign House, where no one was ever allowed to speak—only sign. I chose to live in the hearing world, but after taking Sign Language, Psychology of Deafness, and History of Deafness, I did entertain the notion of becoming an interpreter. But my hand motions were never precise enough. I'd mean to say, "I don't understand" but instead point out someone's cold sore.

Because I knew that good grades alone could not guarantee financial success as a single parent, that summer, while living at home in New York, I attempted a potentially résumé-building internship at an advertising research facility. (My mother and I thought that my interest in commercials could be channeled into marketing analysis.)

Every day, the small staff busily crunched numbers while I sat in a claustrophic cube and flipped through a big black binder nearly half my size, attempting to familiarize myself with the company goals. The dreariness of the numbers and graphs and organization charts and financial estimates, in combination with the uninspiring faint sound of fingers typing and printers printing, made me feel feverish and swollen-glandy. To maintain sanity, I took pleasure in inhaling the metallic smell of my desk lamp, spinning around in my twisty chair, and organizing paper clips into elaborate formations up and down my thigh.

Fridays were dress-down days, when one actually got to put

on jeans and sneakers and show remote signs of individuality. They reminded me of the "nonuniform days" we used to have in grammar school. The faculty got tense on those occasions, as if chaos might ensue because the popular girls were wearing their cowboy boots. I had a sense that the vice presidents of the ad firm saw summer Fridays as similarly risky. If employees actually felt comfortable in their shoes, their accuracy on Excel spreadsheets would surely be compromised.

On summer Fridays, I followed my instinct to rebel and wore short knit shorts with sheer stockings, sneakers, and off-the-shoulder tops. As I'd march into the office, my supervisor's eyes would narrow with disapproval. One Tuesday she called me into her office:

"Wendy. Um, this is a little embarrassing. Shut the door." She folded her legs and tucked her tight brown bob behind both her ears.

"Okay. Oh dear."

"Well, it's nothing that bad. It's just, well, the VPs are . . . profoundly disturbed by the provocative nature of your Friday attire. And your Monday to Thursday attire too, actually. Low-cut blouses and flared pants aren't appropriate 'business casual.' This isn't some disco party. We'll need you to dress more professionally. Do you know what that even means? Have you never been to Banana Republic?"

I gulped and nodded and shuffled away, remembering the time I'd gotten detention in ninth grade for wearing my headband skirt so high that one could see the control tops of my pantyhose. I toned it down after our little talk, but because they seemed to barely need an intern anyway, I spent the rest of my Fridays sleeping in the bathroom stalls. I would rest my head on the well-scented toilet paper and drift off, awaking periodically because my head had rolled off, or because of a particularly loud flush.

One evening toward the end of the summer, on my way home from the office, I saw a wrinkled ad taped to a bus stop. It was for a job being a pretend call-in person for a radio show. (I guess most of the people calling in to share stories on those shows are imposters. Who knew?) Since advertising research was clearly not working out, I signed up as soon as I got home, and was assigned a 7 a.m. gig for the following day.

The next morning the radio producer called the house and woke me up.

"Okay, Wendy, so we are going live in five . . . remember, your name is Dolores, you're from Jersey, and you have been dating this guy for six months."

"Uh huh."

"Okay, and you are really, really pissed at this guy because he got a free set of roses from a flower shop and had it delivered to another woman instead of you. You are really, really pissed . . . curse a lot . . . be really loud. We will bleep out the really dirty words as you talk. Okay, GO!"

It was the crack of dawn, I never yell, my acne mask was still plastered on my face, and I was wearing candy-cane striped footie pajamas. "Um, you motherfucker? You assHOLE! WHO DO YOU THINK I AM? YOU *DONKEY* MOTHERFUCKER!!!"

I came up with that in the moment. "Donkey motherfucker." It was pretty powerful. And somewhat cathartic.

When I called my radio employer the next day, I was disappointed to learn that performing call-ins full time would only pay about a hundred dollars per week and thus not send my kids to private school. I returned to Wesleyan for my senior year with no plan for a postgraduation career path. I was, of course, incredibly panicked about this but kept myself distracted by focusing on my senior thesis.

For a psychology thesis, students could choose to perform an experiment, in which they collected and studied data, or write an intensely researched paper based on previous studies. Ever since my mother had become a sex therapist, I'd been interested in the sexual differences between men and women, so I wrote and analyzed a survey exploring these differences, which I oh-so-cleverly called "Wham, Bam, Thank You, *Sir*." It asked students prying questions about their turn-ons, masturbating practices, and sexual satisfaction. The project entailed rereading my mother's old juicy sex books and dissecting people's private lives—work I felt totally comfortable with. As a bonus, while stuffing envelopes with my survey, I was able to lick, seal, and smell stationery for hours on end.

This is sort of how I met Amos. I was in the computer lab of the science building, devising the first draft of questions, when he came up to me and asked for a piece of gum. I handed him a few gumballs and said, "Hey, would you mind filling out my sex survey, and maybe telling me whether you think it's thorough enough?" I needed objective male feedback, and felt comfortable asking him in particular because he had a very swarthy thing going on. He was tall and built, had thick black hair past his chin, partially covered by a wool cap, a goatee, hoops in both ears, and thick long eyelashes. At the time I was attracted to paler, preppier types without wool caps.

"Your *what*?" he replied, fidgeting with his right earring.

"My sex survey. It's for my psychology thesis. I'm investigating differences in female and male sexuality and I really need advice on it before I distribute."

"I guess . . . well . . . can I see it first?"

I printed out my draft and handed him the twenty-page booklet. After looking at the first question ("How many people have you slept with?"), he shifted his shoulders, scratched his eyebrow, and tentatively sat down at a nearby table to fill the whole thing out. When he handed it back and shyly walked away, I was slightly disturbed. "Nineteen" seemed like a lot of sexual partners for a college senior. *Huh. Slightly sketchy. Well, he must be skilled in the sack. Wait, is he at all attractive? Maybe the swarthiness is attractive.* I scanned the rest of his answers. *Apparently he likes giving oral sex. How much exactly? "Ten" on a scale of one to ten. Interesting.*

For weeks I could not stop imagining Amos in various sexual positions, his hoops glistening in the moonlight and his wool cap flying off his head in a moment of heated passion. When I finally saw him again at a backyard party, we sat on a tree stump and, like two bad actors flirting in soft-core porn, conversed about my sex findings for three hours until we finally went back to his place to roll around under his tapestry. After a couple of sleepovers, I worshiped his natural scent to the point of exhaustion and talked endlessly of capturing it in a sealed bottle for mass production. Soon he would become the most lovable, patient boyfriend of all time—the rare kind who asks endless questions about your day, your job, your family, your friends, and your childhood, and then actually remembers every boring detail.

* * *

Despite the sensitive, sexually skilled new man in my life, and the fact that I'd made it through another four years of school, a few months later, during my graduation ceremony, I was deeply concerned. Rain was pouring down and the dye in my red robe was bleeding onto my favorite dress. Paul Simon (the senator, not the musician) was giving a speech about some political thing I didn't fully understand. And in just a few hours, I would have to enter the real world with no strategy for supporting myself, much less my future children. There was just no way in hell I was ever going to thrive in a world where I'd have to attempt to understand a 401(k).

But I *could* African dance fairly well. And I knew from my survey that 35 percent of female students rarely had orgasms during actual intercourse. And I was extra mad at society for objectifying women. And I had collected a lot of amusing wind-up knickknacks from toy stores in the Connecticut area.

As I took apart my futon, storage crates, and plastic nightstand the next morning, I considered that maybe I wasn't ever going to become a dermatologist, lawyer, or businesswoman. Maybe I was prepared for a life on my own terms, whatever that might be. Even if it meant working a second job and someday sending my kids to public school in Brooklyn, where I'd probably want them to go anyway.

free spatulas

The letter was succinct and ominous:

At the bottom of the high-quality paper was a raised triangular black logo that felt neat against my fingertips.

I had just returned home after college graduation with the desperate hope of finding a job in the city—one that might help me discover what I was supposed to be when I grew up. I was too curious not to follow up on this piece of junk mail, so that Monday morning I put on a black-and-white, sassy-yet-professional Betsey Johnson dress and, armed with mace, arrived at the "main" office—a large room filled with gray fold-out chairs and white rugs covered in questionable stains. There were about thirty of us shuffling about, all roughly the same age and looking equally confused. It was kind of like the movie *Clue*. Everyone was mumbling, "Did you get that *letter*?"

After a significant period of suspense, a young man with far too many blackheads on his forehead made a grand entrance from the bathroom. "Hello! Thank you for coming. You are all probably wondering what this is all about. Well, every single one of you was asked here for the same reason. You were all hardworking students. And as of this very moment, you are on the cusp of the greatest moneymaking opportunity in the history of moneymaking opportunities." For five minutes he ranted about how life was short and how his cousin almost died at twenty-five and *now*, not later, was the time to improve one's standard of living.

Then, like an afterthought under his breath, he mumbled that we were really here to interview for a two-month stint selling knives door-to-door. Kitchen knives, for commission.

People started storming out. The guy waved his arms in the air and pleaded, "If you leave now, you are missing out, folks. You'll regret it!" I've never been able to live with regret, so I stayed in my seat eager to see where this was all going and wondering if he'd ever seen a dermatologist for the blackhead problem.

Ten others hesitantly remained with me. Unshaken by the diminished audience, he clumsily wheeled a TV to the front of the room and played a ten-minute tape introducing us to the marketing company involved in the venture. There were endless testimonials from a diverse group of young adults. "Knife-selling changed everything. It provided marketing experience far more valuable than any expensive business degree." "These knives sell themselves. All I had to do was show up." "Thank goodness I opened that letter and was introduced to the world of knife-selling. God knows what kind of degenerate I'd be if I hadn't attended and stayed for the entire duration of that initial meeting."

The guy shut the power off, paused, and frowned. "Now, not everyone can just automatically join our company," he said, tapping one of his blackheads. "We look for *super-duper stars*, not just hardworking students. I'll need to interview you one by one now in the corner area. Wendy Spero, you're first up. Dave Freedman, you're on deck."

I proceeded to the folding chair in the back corner area while the rest of the group watched suspiciously from the other side of the room. He asked me where I had gone to school and what I had studied.

"I went to Wesleya—"

"I think you have something darn special, Wendy. I'd love for you to come aboard. Congratulations! Please stick around for the next portion of the meeting."

I was slightly traumatized by having to look at his black-heads up close but was thrilled to have made the cut. I didn't want to make the others envious, though, so I put on a neutral face and swaggered back to my seat.

One by one, we were all formally accepted into this highly selective marketing conglomerate. Then he lined up some knives onto a few chairs facing us, and announced that we'd have to buy an initial knife kit for one hundred dollars.

As the girl next to me stood up, she whispered, "Get OUT! This is a scam!" But I looked at the shiny cutlery and thought, *I must sell knives.*

Eventually, only two of us were left. The other woman was wearing braces—the clear kind that turn yellow over time. We handed the man credit cards and left with pounds of merchandise and a new purpose in life.

When I immediately informed friends and family that I'd found the perfect summer job, they responded with stilted enthusiasm. I think they worried that I had joined a cult and would soon be wearing a flowy skirt and handing out dandelions next to the Holland Tunnel.

The following weekend, Lucy, my best friend from high school, invited me to her family's rented summerhouse in Martha's Vineyard so I could reboot before officially starting. Because we spent every moment at the beach, and I was never motivated to put on sunscreen, I got a *severe* burn on my face. Big red chunks of my skin dangled. I looked like I was in one of those old ABC after-school specials based on a horrible true story, like I'd been burned in a fire by an evil stepmother or something.

Because my face felt so insanely hot, when we smoked weed that Saturday night, it was as though I were experiencing the evening's events from the bong's point of view. I alone could identify with the burning herbs on the receiving end of a pothead's inhale. It was deep.

When I returned to the city, I rushed to the dermatologist, who could barely hide her fearful reaction to my appearance. She prescribed a soothing white steroid cream for the swelling, and two days later I grew a spontaneous mustache. A little prickly Fu Manchu one.

So I had the mustache, the burn, and a sack o' knives.

I was ready to sell.

The knife-selling process was a safe, meticulously thought-out scheme. Per the instructions in my knife-selling packet, I called my mom's good, trustworthy friends and politely asked for some names and numbers of their good, trustworthy friends. I then called these people up and performed a well-rehearsed, innocent shtick: "Hi, so, um, so-and-so told me you would be nice enough to help me out. I'm learning about marketing and wondered if I could come over to your house maybe for just a couple minutes and practice selling . . . *things* . . . to you."

Each sucker would reply, "Oh sure dear, that's sweet. Well, I'm not going to buy anything, but sure—if you want *practice.*" Shortly thereafter I'd arrive at their apartment. They'd open the door, notice my deformity, and mutter, "Oh. Oh my. Oh dear. Have you tried *aloe*?"

I'd sit at their kitchen table and compliment their hair. We'd gab about our friend in common. Then I'd commence the mind-blowing presentation: I'd slice brown leather into strips with steak knives. I'd cut a thick rope with a bread knife. In one fluid motion, I'd cut a penny in half with large silver shears. (A thrill in and of itself because cutting currency is technically a federal offense.) I'd revel in the subtle sound of every long, deep, satisfying incision.

At first my customers would act condescending, politely nodding and mumbling, "Uh huh, yeah, uh huh." But as the presentation progressed, they'd find themselves seeking clarification. "Wait, hold on. How much is that one again?" There was simply no way to remain unaffected by my slick marketing moves.

I was also prepared for the toughest of customer questions. They'd ask, "But wait, if your knives are that sharp, aren't they dangerous?" Unfazed, I'd grin and explain that actually, using one of their *dull* knives was far more risky. "Statistics show that chefs are 46 percent more likely to slip while cutting a tomato from a worn down blade."

They'd let out a contemplative, "Huh. Wow. Yeah."

To close the sale I'd lean in, signal for them to lean in, look around (there would only be two of us in the apartment), and whisper, "You know what? I'm not supposed to do this, but I'll give you a free spatula with that bread knife. How's that?" A tiny bit would come out of my commission, but they'd fall for it every time—they'd end up buying an entire set, which they didn't even need in the first place, just to get something for free. Then we'd hug. They'd thank me profusely, and I'd leave with seven hundred of their dollars.

I was thrilled to be good at a real grown-up job, and I didn't feel guilty because at the biweekly knife meetings, the convincing blackhead leader explained over and over again that by selling people these knives, we were massively improving their lives—even if they didn't cook. I was making the world a better place.

I even preyed on our dearest of family friends. My friend Emily recalls her mother telling the family at breakfast that I'd be coming over that afternoon to practice selling "things," and that she might go ahead and buy one item—just to be nice. Later that evening, as the family talked about their days at the dining room table, her father asked, "Oh, so did Wendy come over? Did you end up buying something to be nice?" Emily's mom fell silent. She had spent over two thousand dollars on *knives* she didn't remotely need. "Look. Stop hounding me. I don't know what happened." She moaned. "She . . . she cut leather and then pennies and . . . and I just lost all control. They seemed really necessary at the time . . . I swear . . . We got a free spatula!?"

While I calculated purchase totals and filled out the necessary forms, my clients would happily write down twenty or so names and numbers of friends I could contact. I would call those people up, do the shtick, sell them knives, ask for names, and so on and so on. After three or four weeks I had been to so many houses that I had no memory of the original round of victims. I'd call some random guy and say, "Hi, Mary Bingham recommended that I contact you. She said you might be nice enough to help me out . . ." all the while having no clue who Mary was. Then I'd arrive at his door and chat with him for a solid fifteen minutes about Mary's terrific new gig in the meatpacking district. After noticing the words "cute dog" next to Mary's name on my special knife-selling pad, I'd be sure to add, "And wow, Mary's dog is something, huh?"

Eventually, I started getting calls from people desperately *seeking* knives. "Hello, um, I heard you are a knife expert and you come directly to people's houses . . . can you fit me in? I know you must be so busy. Please. I hear you are the best. I don't trust those pushy salespeople in stores. Salespeople are the worst, ya know?"

Sometimes between appointments I would take a break and wander into a big clothing store like Urban Outfitters. Upon passing through the metal detectors, the entire alarm system would go off. The guard would ask, "Uh, ma'am, what do you have in your bag?" I'd reply, "Knives." He would laugh, and let me in. I was invincible.

The sale of the century occurred one Tuesday afternoon when a friend of a friend of a friend asked me to meet her at her office. As I exited the elevator and walked through the corporate glass double doors, a middle-aged receptionist asked, "Can I help—oh! Are *you* the knife woman?"

"I . . . guess?"

She led me to an enormous conference hall with a stage, got on an intercom, and announced: "Attention employees. The knife demonstration will commence in five minutes." *Three hundred* people then poured into the space, and a small fellow with a bow tie got up and bellowed, "With no further ado . . . the floor is *yours*. Do your thang!"

"Heh. All right . . . right . . . okay!" I began. "So, you guys ever cut a tomato and find that the skin gets all mushed?!"

"FUCK YEAH!" yelled the crowd.

Beyond energized, I took out the leather strip and smoothly cut it into thinner strips. I took out the penny and dramatically cut it in half. I took out the impressive bread knife and sliced my left thumb.

Blood was everywhere.

A man shrieked, "Holy—you need to go to the emergency room?"

"Not at all!" I called out nonchalantly. I grabbed a towel from my bag, wrapped it around my hand, held it above my head, applied the necessary pressure, and continued the presentation. And made a fortune.

I was relieved when the summer started to come to an end—my back ached from schlepping around the heavy mass of metal, and my fingers were covered in Band-Aids. But in order to go out with a bang, a week after my big sale I decided to fly to the annual knife-selling convention in Indianapolis, where I was greeted by large posters of rainbows that read, "Fulfill your potential. Persuade! Sell! Conquer!" At the award ceremony that evening I won a tall trophy AND a VCR for selling *the most knives* in the tristate area.

apt. 6c

It was time to move out. I was twenty-three years old and had been living at home with my mother for more than a year after graduating from college. The one-bedroom apartment was feeling increasingly claustrophobic. I was working as a temp while still frantically trying to figure out what I wanted to do with my life, and Mom's passionate pleas for me to still consider becoming a lawyer, dermatologist, or business-woman weren't helping.

I decided to move in with my dear college friend Sumi (not the same person as my dear childhood friend Soomee—how weird is that?) and our other college friend Joanna, who were already living in a mildly grimy, three-bedroom, sixth-floor walk-up on Ninety-sixth Street between Lexington and Park avenues in Manhattan. The apartment was still close to Mom, and it was a relatively good-sized space for a reasonable price, with the benefit of a built-in gym—the six flights up felt never-ending, straight out of an M. C. Escher print. By the time you reached our bristly welcome mat, you were gasping for oxygen and confident that your metabolism had been slightly improved.

The boiler for the building was located in the basement, but its gurgling sounds were so powerful that every couple of hours we'd hear a resounding *urghgggxxtt*. Because the groan sounded a little like the rumblings of acid indigestion, we called the boiler Pepta. Naming the boiler made the noise less frightening. It helped us think of it as a pet living below some secret trap door. "There's goes Pepta again. Settle down, Pepta. Settle down."

When Sumi and Joanna eventually moved out a year later to go to law school, I signed a new lease and was given the task of filling the two vacancies. Sumi let me keep her torn college furniture for the common area, which I decorated with a furry rug and a stained placemat/wall hanging that said "Wendy's Place." (It was an old party favor from someone's bat mitzvah.) I also took over the largest bedroom, where I had the space to run wild with an elaborate finger puppet display.

The move came at the peak of my finger puppet phase, which had begun a few months earlier, after I had what I thought was a profoundly entertaining realization: if you give someone the finger, but do so while wearing a happy ladybug or mailman finger puppet, the harsh meaning is lessened. Instead of "Fuck you!" you're saying, "You're a meanie!"

Since then, I'd been conducting biweekly visits to a finger puppet/pottery store in Brooklyn, conveniently located a block from Amos's house.

The first time I saw their handmade wool finger puppet designs in the window, I lost all control. When ringing me up, the saleswoman remarked, "Um . . . ma'am, you have seventy-five dollars worth of finger puppets here." I replied, "And your point is?"

I ultimately collected a total of about fifty of these puppets, which included both animals and people in various occupational uniforms (a nurse, a policeman, a king, a zookeeper, a pilot, etc.). I came to think of them as portable stuffed animals, and began sticking one or two of them in my pant pocket before leaving the house. One Saturday, when I picked up my stack of neatly folded laundry from the corner cleaners, a warm, bright-eyed bumblebee finger puppet lay comfortably at the top of the pile, his wings carefully folded over the rubber band used to tie the clothes together. To this day I still wonder what the elderly Korean woman thought when she organized my clothes that day. Had she been in the business so long that nothing remotely surprised her? Was it all run of the mill? (Remove jeans from dryer and fold, remove undershirt from dryer and fold, remove bee finger puppet, fold wings . . .) Or did she do it as a "wink wink, I'm in on your weird fetish" thing?

Anyway, in order to create a professional setup in my new master bedroom, I convinced the owner of the pottery store to sell me the small wooden hands that they'd used to prop up the puppets. As a supplement, Amos built a multilayered stand out of Lego for ten of my favorites. They were arranged like nursery school kids posing for an important class photo—three lines, with the shortest puppets in front. Because all school pictures include a sign, I wrote "Puppet Class '99" on a small cardboard square and gave it to the lucky goat in front row center to hold. The display made me smile on a daily basis. Most important, however, it became a crucial component of the roommate screening process.

After sending out a mass "roommate wanted" e-mail to friends, I arranged to meet with twenty twentysomethings who were looking for a cheap room uptown. (I talked to thirty people on the phone, but instantly eliminated ten because of their grating voices.) By the time each candidate rang the doorbell, they'd be completely winded and drenched in sweat. I'd immediately offer a cold glass of water, a paper towel, and a seat on the yarny couch. Once they recovered from the work-out, I'd make the side-splitting joke about the advantage of a free built-in gym, and lead them through the hallway, kitchen, and bathroom while walking backward with my hands motioning as if I were a museum guide. Inevitably, Pepta would gaseously growl, and I'd have to explain that the boiler was temperamental but friendly. Then, the tour would come to a sudden, final halt at the finger puppet display.

"And finally . . . here are my *finger puppets.*"

This was a key moment. To me, the candidate's reaction to my collection was directly proportional to how cool they'd be to live with. If they were anything less than enthusiastic, they'd automatically get bumped from the master list.

My system proved to be slightly imperfect after I offered the room on the spot to a curly haired filmmaker who promised to cast my finger puppets in his upcoming project. He saw star potential, and we spent nearly an hour brainstorming ideas. "What if we had them act out scenes from actual movies with real audio in the background?" I suggested. "We could shoot the little ladybug crouched over sobbing in a mini-bathtub, pretending to be Glenn Close in *The Big Chill.*"

When he gushed over the idea, it was clear that we were on the same page, and he asked to move into both of the two available rooms, so he could convert the larger one into a film studio. He was willing to pay two rents.

To say I was thrilled beyond belief is an understatement. We made arrangements for him to move in the following weekend. He e-mailed me the next morning to thank me again for everything, and we had a few witty, borderline-flirty exchanges. But when he suggested we meet for a late-night dinner at his favorite obscure Thai place—forty blocks from the apartment—to hammer out logistical details, I worried he was asking me out on a date. But, no, that was unlikely, because he was a smart, perceptive guy, and I had purposely mentioned Amos on numerous occasions, and if he really were interested in dating me, he'd have to be really, really stupid to want the room because everyone knows that moving into a stranger's small Manhattan tenement is not a way into her pants.

When I updated Amos on the situation, he acted annoyingly unboyfriend-like. "Well, I dunno, I think he's probably just being nice and grateful. If he's really willing to pay for two rents, just let him move in and be done with the search. Anyway, his desire to re-create scenes from *Into the Woods* with finger cozies suggests he might be gay."

I ignored Amos, listened to my womanly instinct, which had become increasingly suspicious, and called the curly haired filmmaker to say that Sumi had unexpectedly returned to New York and needed both rooms. He took the news well, and we agreed this would only be a minor hiccup in the making of our award-winning finger puppet movie.

Two minutes later he e-mailed me an insanely flirty message saying that my voice turned him on, and that living apart was for the best because now we could date like a proper couple. I did not respond. Instead I forwarded the e-mail to Amos to prove that the flirtation hadn't been in my head, and that I was right to go against his horrendously offensive advice.

Within seconds of forwarding the message the following e-mail popped up on my screen.

To: jaemes1@yahoo.com
Bcc: Wendy Spero
From: Amos Elliston

Hey dickhead,
Wendy has a boyfriend.
—Amos (her boyfriend)

Amos had e-mailed the guy *directly*. I cannot express how uncharacteristic this was of him. He had never shown even remote signs of jealousy. To the point of being troubling. A day earlier he'd been in favor of me living with a guy who might have crept into my room at night, decorated me with goat finger puppets, and taken pictures to post on some sick porn site. I called Amos and yelled, "What were you thinking? I didn't mean to get him in trouble! I was just making a point!" He argued, "Fuck that. How dare he hit on my girlfriend." I felt bad for the guy, but was definitely turned on by Amos's newfound manly assertiveness.

The following day, like a gift from the heavens, I got a call at one of my office temp jobs. "Hi . . . um . . . A friend sent me your housing e-mail. I heard you were really nice and normal. That is so great. My name is Irene. I'm really nice and really normal too . . . I was on *The Real World*."

As if being on MTV's *The Real World* was proof of normalcy.

I hadn't ever really watched *The Real World*, so I put her on hold and ran to my friend's cube screaming, "Do you remember an Irene from the Seattle *Real World*?!" She was like, "OH MY GOD. That girl is totally famous! She had to leave the show for going completely crazy after getting Lyme disease! There was this one bizarre episode where this mean guy slapped her in the face for being such a crazy housemate."

I rushed back to the phone and gasped, "Wanna come over tonight?" The person known from national television for being the worst possible roommate EVER was trying to be my roommate.

Yesss.

So she came over, and, like a spy, I went through my normal routine while extracting key information that I could take back to my coworkers. "And here is the bathroom . . . there are a lot of shelves in the cabinet here . . . in case you take a lot of pills . . . so it is true you had health issues on the show?" She explained that Lyme disease can affect your mind but that her medication had helped significantly and that she had been lecturing on the college circuit about media manipulation. She claimed she'd been wrongly depicted on the MTV series. She also said she was interested in the room, but, unfortunately, blew me off the following week after a couple rounds of phone tag.

It was nearing the end of the month, and I could not afford to pay the next month's full rent. I frantically called the back-up candidates—despite their grating voices—retired the finger puppet screening process, and threw caution to the wind.

From that point on, I became something like a mother hen of the apartment, overseeing a constant rotation of what seemed like a thousand wacko roommates over the next six years.

At one point I took in an older woman named Barbara who wore a lot of beaded ankle socks with moccasins. I never once saw her leave her room. At the same time, I also took in a girl who had just graduated from her hometown college in Idaho. I'd rather not use her real name, but let's just say it was unusual, and a noun relating to an insignificant body of water. I'll refer to her as Puddle.

Puddle was utterly virginal and naturally stunning. She was five foot nine and voluptuous, with piercing brown eyes, the clearest skin I'd ever seen, and long, braided auburn hair down to her butt—it had never, ever been cut. Puddle had come to New York for the first time, with the hope of working for any company remotely connected to Gloria Estefan, who had been her idol since childhood.

As one might expect, Puddle was initially anxious about her new independence. Every night she'd lock, unlock, and relock the door, and ask me things like, "Are you sure the door is closed *completely*? Could men be looking in through the cracks in my wavy blinds with binoculars? Can blinds be ironed?" But after only two weeks there was a radical change. I'd walk through the door, and she'd yelp, "Wendy! I feel like Gloria Estefan! So many guys were looking at me on the subway today! Just now someone whistled at me when I walked by that construction site. How do I get them to ask for my number?" We'd be quietly watching TV at midnight—I'd be half asleep—and some dopey spokesman would come on selling vacuum cleaners. He'd bend down to pull a cord, and she'd shock me into consciousness by suddenly screaming, "GIMME A PIECE A THAT!"

By the third week Puddle had started an intense love affair with the forty-five-year-old Albanian deli man from downstairs. She had offered her cell number one afternoon after he handed her a bunch of change. Despite the fact that he barely spoke English, they would gab for hours on the phone. I'd hear her describe the intricacies of her love for Gloria without pausing. She'd also ask him about the status of his relationship with his wife and kids.

I was worried for Puddle, but it was helpful having an "in" at the deli. We were able to buy toilet paper hours after the store had officially closed. She'd also bring home piles of free, sliced turkey breast.

I even began to enjoy my role as the official advisor for Puddle's blossoming sexuality. As I dragged myself out of bed one Tuesday morning at 7 a.m., Puddle walked into the kitchen and whispered, "Hey Wendy . . . I know it's early but . . . how do you know if you have an orgasm?"

"I think you'd know."

"I can't tell. Last night we were necking at his friend's place . . . we had our clothes on but were rubbing our crotches together. We started rubbing incredibly fast and then, all of a sudden, I wanted to go to sleep. And my legs jerked a little like a half-dead fish. Do you think that was one?"

I felt a little nauseated but was able to muster up a "maybe."

Then I bought her *Our Bodies, Ourselves* and handed her an extra copy of my college sex thesis.

When Puddle moved out the following spring to live with her cousin in New Jersey, she was replaced with a guy, who (God's honest truth) referred to himself by the nickname Bushy Tush. Bushy Tush was a friend of a coworker and had come highly recommended. He had a long, brown greasy ponytail and a faux British accent. When I asked where he was from he proudly replied, "Everywhere." He was a singer/songwriter in his late thirties who spent a majority of his time performing in small-town musicals across the country. "I'll be away ten out of twelve months of the year," he said. "I'll just send you the rent from wherever I am at the time." He assured me that he was ready to pay for at least two years or more because as a nomad he desperately needed a "base," somewhere he could keep all his stuff and call home.

On his moving-in day, Bushy Tush arrived carrying a small knapsack and a paper bag filled with socks and magazines. "Hello home!" he beamed.

When I asked him when his stuff was arriving he said, "This is it. I'm a minimalist."

"So, um, well, do you need a bed?"

"I could totally use one, actually."

"Well, I guess you could take the extra futon mattress in my room."

"See? This was meant to be. Hey, I could also use a shower. How's the water pressure?"

"Not bad."

"Got any towels lying around?"

"Uh . . . sure. I guess you can just use the blue one on the hook in there."

"Perfection."

When I got home from work the next night Bushy Tush was lying on the living room couch in my blue towel. *SportsCenter* was blaring. Instead of lowering the volume he yelled, "WEL-COME HOME, WEN. SO YOU SHOULD KNOW—NEXT WEEK I'M OUTA HERE UNTIL EARLY SEPTEMBER. I'M OFF TO DO CLASSICAL MUSICAL PANTOMIME IN NE-BRASKA!"

The following week he left for Nebraska with the knapsack and paper bag, closing his bedroom door behind him. For weeks, I'd walk by and wonder how my futon was doing in there. Eventually I was concerned he was stashing a dead body. I didn't want to invade his privacy, though, and as long as he was paying for it, the room was his to stash whatever he wanted.

Two months later, Barbara packed up her beaded ankle socks and moccasins and fled to her parents' house in Texas. Once again, I needed to fill the vacancy and conduct the same old roommate tour, but this time without showing Bushy Tush's bedroom. I'd explain to various candidates, "Uh . . . and there's the other bedroom. The guy doesn't live here really, so you probably won't have to ever see him, although he's supposed to be back in September, but just for a bit." There might as well have been one of those fluorescent "caution" police ribbons across his door. Luckily, Nicole, Amos's perfectly nice, quiet coworker didn't seem to mind and came aboard.

Bushy Tush had started sending me his rent mid-month in the form of checks he received for numerous gigs. Since he didn't have a checking account, I felt weird taking his money. When he'd call to tell me the rent was on its way, I'd reply, "Are you sure you can afford this? You are putting all your money toward a room you don't use." He'd just reiterate his desperate need for a "base," one in which he could store all his "stuff." It was almost too sad to be interesting. But my friend who had referred him assured me that he was a successful, working singer/songwriter who loved his life.

Two years later, when Nicole announced she was leaving for grad school that summer, I decided I'd had enough. I'd spent nearly a fifth of my adulthood convincing friends of friends of friends that Pepta was endearing and that six flights of stairs wasn't that bad, all to keep an unimpressive, claustrophobic flat. Plus, after being together for almost seven years, it was time for Amos and me to move in together in Brooklyn. When I called Bushy Tush to give him the news, he was in shock. "But my base! That is my *base*. What about my stuff? Okay, okay. But promise to send me my stuff. *Promise*."

After I had cleaned up the six years' worth of crap that had accumulated in the apartment, I was forced to bust into Bushy Tush's room to gather his said belongings. When I removed my hands from my eyes, I saw no dead bodies. Instead I saw a crack den without the crack. A stained futon covered with matches, wrinkly navy socks, bits of paper, pens without caps, and bread crumbs. Next to the bed was my old towel, and on top of the towel was a high pile of used, crumpled tissues, and next to the mound were twenty, empty miniature moisturizer bottles from Best Western.

Yes. The guy had been paying rent for his DNA to reside on the Upper East Side. I was honestly surprised I hadn't walked in to find an infant who had been born spontaneously from too much concentrated sperm.

But I'd promised him his "stuff," so once the initial shock wore off, I swept the whole mess into a big square carton. The movers accidentally picked up the box and brought it to our new clean place in Park Slope. I was so disgusted/amused when I later opened what I thought would be a package full of wineglasses that I choked on my gum. But I pulled myself together, retaped the flaps, and sent Bushy Tush his splooge via UPS Second Day. I completed the last of my duties as mother hen of Apt. 6C.

how cool is my mom?

In a predicament? Call my mom.

A few years ago, while I was still living in Apt. 6C, I was all set to start a permanent administrative assistant day job to accompany the beginnings of a stand-up career. (Performing on a stage seemed like a way to re-create the fun of knife demonstrations, only with less risk of physical harm.) But then I heard from the HR woman that the company required a drug test before you could officially begin. I had been smoking pot every weekend since college and worried I'd never pass. Amos had heard of a thick, grainy, yellow liquid that you could drink to flush your system of traces of marijuana and purchased a bottle at the nearby health food store. On the cap, in bold, red letters, it read "May cause gagging reflex." Since I get indigestion at the drop of a hat, I thought I would just skip the potion, avoid gagging, take the test, and hope for the best. If I failed, so be it. But Amos thought there might be a big, mean puritanical database somewhere that kept track of all the innocent druggies who fail these sorts of things, and that, once you were in the system, the government could come and drag you away in squeaky chains to a dark pit full of lepers when you least expected it. I started to panic, and did what I always do in a bind:

"Mom, I have a problem."

"I'm listening . . ."

"I need to take a drug test for the stupid job. And, well, you know, I mean, I don't think I'll pass, right? Which is fine, I mean, ugh, it's so wrong to drug test, right? But should I not take it? I mean, what if there is a massive database that stores this sort of information and it's used against me somehow in the future?"

Mom had already accepted that I was somewhat of a marijuana fan. During my postcollege year living at home, she would often walk through my room, smell basily fumes, roll her eyes to the right, scrunch her lips into a wrinkly knot to the left, and let out a soft groan of reluctant tolerance. "Wendaay," she'd say. "Just don't get addicted like those kids I once saw on *Dateline.*"

It seemed like ages since the days when I was glad my mom wasn't the type of "cool" parent that was totally lax about drugs and alcohol; now I was glad that she had adjusted her views as I'd grown up. Still, a drug test seemed like a big thing for a parent to digest, and I worried that she might be mad about all the pot smoking, and/or about it potentially compromising the job. Instead, she took a deep breath and announced, "I'M ON IT!"

My mom then called me back every thirty minutes. "Just wanting to let you know, I'm still ON IT. I've put in a lot of calls. I'm networking."

I was consumed with guilt and pleaded, "Mom, really, don't spend all your time on this. It's fine, whatever. It's just an administrative assistant job for the money. You're busy. I was just asking your advice." But my infinitely devoted mother couldn't focus on anything else, and a week later her hard work paid off. Through her various connections in the field of psychology and substance abuse, she had somehow managed to get a meeting with the HEAD of drug testing for the *NFL.*

The following Tuesday she called me from his office. I could hear the man talking beside her.

Mom: Wendaay, I'm in the meeting! HOLD ON. He has questions.

NFL Dude: So how much pot does she smoke?

Mom (earnestly repeating into the phone): So how much pot do you smoke?

Me (ashamed): I smoke a lot of pot.

Mom (addressing the man): She smokes a lot of pot.

NFL Dude: Well has she done coke recently?

Mom (into the receiver, all matter-of-factly): Well have you done coke recently?

(Long pause.)

Me (highly disturbed): Oh. Um, oy. I just tried a *little* coke on New Year's for the first time.

Mom (to the man): She did coke on New Year's. Yup. Yes, sir. Affirmative on the coke!

The head of drug testing then explained that although a thorough drug test could most definitely reveal cocaine use if taken within the month, there was no such thing as a central database and the government would not come and hunt me down in twenty years. Also, the grainy yellow potion would probably not make a difference and would definitely give me gas.

I decided to just drink twenty glasses of water the night before the test.

After passing with flying colors, the first thing I had to do was share the news with my mother.

"Mom. I passed!"

"Wendaay. I'm so proud of you. Congratulations, honey!" I honestly think she'd completely forgotten the real reason behind the test in the first place.

That night she had me over for a celebratory Cornish game hen and even though I was completely sober, her perfectly sweet/sour, dill-flavored marmalade glaze never tasted so good.

why i ended up buying the most hideously bulbous down jacket of all time

Last year, despite my best intentions, I ended up buying the Most Hideously Bulbous Down Jacket of All Time. The "breathable" water-resistant outer layer is the color of a black-and-blue mark—not quite navy, not quite black, just a nasty place in between. "HEAD," the brand name, is written in all caps across the chest, and the sleeves and waist are tapered with Velcro (so snow can't get inside). Because there is no stitching in the poofy body area, there is also an uneven distribution of feathers. If I tilt to the side, a majority of the jacket goes with me. When I wear this jacket, friends are ashamed to be seen with me, especially because I prefer wearing it with a triangular, rainbow-colored wool hat that ties tightly under the chin.

Why did I end up with this jacket? Because of a fancy phone I was given at age ten.

Just months before my tenth birthday, I saw a TV commercial for a phone called Private Call: The Phone of Your *Own*. A teenager with a brunette bob was gabbing on the phone in her teenagery room when a short, sweaty boy—her annoying younger brother, I guess—busted in, grabbed the receiver, and tried to prank one of the friends saved on her speed dial. After the teenage girl yelled, "Give it back! Get out, brat!" there were magnificent shots of a special product, the answer to all of her problems. It was a large, pearly white rectangular phone with a handset, keypad, and five-slot photo album. There was also a big porcelain-looking flap attached via a hinge on the right side. Apparently, the lucky owner of this apparatus could not only store five images of friends, along with their numbers, but could also fold the flap over the keypad and pictures and lock it with a heart-shaped key, so no one else could have access. (If the phone was locked, you could answer it, but not dial out.)

Despite the fact that I was an only child who rarely talked on the phone, I knew this product would guarantee success and happiness for life, and begged for it every day until my birthday. And on March 20, 1985, thanks to my mom, I became a proud owner. At last I could see pictures of my friends when I spoke to them at night (which was never) and hide speed dial buttons from the sneaky younger sibling I didn't have.

After the initial elation wore off, the phone's features sent me into a profound state of indecision. I simply could not decide which numbers to program and what order to put them in. At first I plugged 911 into button number one, mom's work number into number two, my grandparents into number three, and Maya into number four. But then I realized there was no picture for "emergency" and figured 9-1-1 was easy to type in directly if necessary. So I had to reprogram mom into number one, grandparents into number two, Maya into number three, and Soomee into number four. But then I panicked that Soomee might come over and see that she was below Maya in the order. And then I couldn't find a good snapshot of my grandparents without red-eye. And did I need to take a picture of my mother at her office or could I use one from Thanksgiving? I had to be excessively thorough because I knew there was one right combination out there. If I found it, I would experience perfect phone bliss, and if I didn't, I'd always wonder what might have been.

My distress over the phone's options only got worse. As I got older and found that talking on the phone for hours about nothing was crucial to my existence, new friends would come over and get pissed if the phone was open and their name was absent from the auto-dial list. ("You have Lucy on your phone and not me? I thought we were closer than you and Lucy.") There was also the issue of concealing the key. I'd put it under a plant, but realize that any dope would guess "under the plant." In the Monopoly box? No, it might be mistaken for a piece and we'd already lost the shoe and the horseman. Again and again and again, I'd decide to put the key somewhere, then change my mind and rehide it. Sometimes I'd forget where I'd stashed it, and for months we'd be unable to make calls from my room.

Private Call sent me into such a whirlwind of uncertainty on so many levels that I eventually entered a dark vortex of indecision from which I have yet to escape. When the phone eventually broke years later, I figured that the worst was over. Surely life would get less complicated going forward. But, surprisingly enough, I continued to be bombarded by choices, and picking paths became exponentially more paralyzing.

And it's the worst with shopping.

Every purchase has to be thoroughly researched and every employee at every store is forced to express his or her opinion and eventually vote. And because employees can be biased (they might be working on commission), I also demand advice from innocent shoppers who have better things to do with their time than help me figure out whether to buy the small or the medium. Or whether a one-shouldered Tarzany shirt is too trendy, or genuinely stunning in an ironic, self-aware kind of way.

The madness reached an all-time high this past winter when it got way too cold in New York, and I desperately needed to take the plunge from wool coat to thick down jacket.

I woke up early one Saturday morning in December and I went to six discount designer stores around Manhattan with notable cold-weather selections. Because it was impossible to accurately assess matters under their unflattering fluorescent lighting, I figured I'd go ahead and purchase numerous jackets with the intention of picking one in the privacy of my own home and returning the rest. But by the end of the weekend I found myself totally debilitated by eight options in varying styles and colors sprawled across my living room floor. The selection looked like a diverse group of cold, faceless people passed out holding hands. Some were intensely warm and sporty, with unnecessary pockets for storing stuff like Cliff bars, and others were more flattering and snow-bunnyish, with drawstrings to cinch in the waist and create an hourglass figure. In my paralysis, I called my mother, who suggested I "go with my gut." Because my gut refused to voice an opinion, I weighed the pros and cons of each option. *If I keep the cute, maroon extra-small Eddie Bauer one, I may feel significantly more attractive day to day, and therefore feel more confident day to day, and therefore become more successful in life. But because it doesn't allow room for many layers underneath, I may get chills if the temperature drops and, as a result, catch a cold, which might eventually grow into a long-term mono-type illness, which might make me chronically tired and therefore less successful in life.*

I dedicated my entire Sunday evening to trying on each jacket five or six times. With a thick sweater. With a thick sweater and a fleece. With a fleece alone. With a turtleneck. And like I do with all totally inconsequential decisions, I made it virtually impossible for Amos to help.

Me: AMOS! Please. Which do I pick?
Amos: I'd rather not get into this with you. You're just going to overanalyze and you're not going to listen to my advice anyway.

Me: Amos! I promise not to overanalyze. Just tell me what you think already.

Amos: Fine. I like the maroon Eddie Bauer one.

Me: But it may not be warm enough. I can barely fit a thick sweater underneath.

Amos: Well then choose the hooded Bloomingdale's one.

Me: But the maroon one is significantly cuter. The hood is bulky. Isn't it important that I look remotely attractive?

Amos: I said the maroon originally. Keep the maroon.

Me: You think appearance is more important than health? Is it really worth the risk? I'll just be sick all the time.

Amos: I don't want you to be sick. Just keep the warmer one then and that's it.

Me: But I'm barely outside that much anyway. I'm in cabs and subways. I could get overheated and uncomfortably sweaty. Hey, what about that super-bulbous one over there on the right?

Amos: That one is hideous. But really, any of them would be fine, babe. You can't go wrong. It's not a big deal.

Me: It is a big deal, Amos. I could be sick all the time or look like a balloon from the Macy's Thanksgiving Day Parade. Fine. Be prepared to either catch a killer cold from me, or think I'm frumpy and gross.

Amos: Looking forward to it.

All of the trying on and pacing back and forth got me overheated, and the subsequent lightheadedness impaired my judgment. Suddenly, all I wanted to do was lie down on a pillow. I found myself swaying back and forth like a buoy, staring bleary-eyed at the choices and craving extreme puffiness. Extreme puffiness called out to me. "Wendy, pick extreme puffiness." Sadly, extreme puffiness could only be found in the option on the right that I'd barely considered all along: the Most Hideously Bulbous Down Jacket of All Time.

Talk about regret. Aside from looking like a freak in the jacket, the bulbousness actually prevents me from doing anything that requires the use of my arms, like picking up a heavy grocery bag or holding onto a railing. The jacket could very well be leading me and my loved ones down a path of doom. I mean, what if the jacket prevents me from successfully waving my arm to grab a cab one night, and that makes me incredibly late to a dinner date with Amos, and that causes him to fill up on bread, and that causes him to order a simple Greek salad instead of a main course, and that causes him to choke on an olive?

I can never wear that jacket again.

The only time I can remember not being totally debilitated by shopping indecision was when Amos and I purchased our blue striped couch from Crate and Barrel two years ago. Our decision was easy for two reasons:

1. Amos and I were completely exhausted when we got to the warehouse in the West Village. Since his father and stepmother were visiting New York and agreed to split the price with us, we had to meet them there at 9 a.m. on a Sunday morning after partying all night. We plopped from one couch to the next, practically dozing off every time. But when we fell into a blue striped sofa, we were deeply enveloped by the material and knew it was the one. (While I recommend buying a couch or a bed when you're tired, do NOT go to a sex shop when you're horny. Seriously, you have no idea what kind of stuff you might end up with. Make a list. *Stick* to the list.)

2. We didn't have to make a full commitment right away. Because we agreed that the couch might be too big for our doorway, we signed up for a "mock delivery." Yes. Apparently this is a fairly common furniture store practice. Crate and Barrel literally comes to your house with a pretend version of your chosen couch in order to make sure it will fit, and you don't actually have to commit to the purchase until you've seen an imitation next to your coffee table and irreplaceable lamp.

The Mock seemed like a solution to all my problems. The concept alone gave me a warm feeling all over, and I made sure to take off work to witness the whole shebang firsthand. I felt like we were all in a play, acting out the scene of an anticipated couch delivery. I even wore a mock turtleneck to get fully into the spirit.

To my surprise, the mock movers did not use a cardboard copy of our couch, but instead came with an actual wool version. No wonder they were so unfriendly and half-assed about it. I've often thought that the job of a mover would be a difficult one—hauling someone else's shit up and down stairs and in and out of vans for hours—but being a *mock* mover would be even worse. You wouldn't even get the satisfaction of actually putting the furniture *down*.

These guys were really unhappy, though, even for overworked, underpaid mock movers. They came halfway up the stairs and said, "Good enough?" I'm not a stickler for these sorts of details but had to reply, "Well, no, really, isn't the point to see if it fits through the doorway?"

They finally agreed to go all of the way inside, but fumed with utter disgust the whole time. I handed them forty dollars, even though I felt like giving them a mock tip.

While the mock delivery was slightly underwhelming, I'd recommend it in a heartbeat. Three months later, when the real movers began to lift the massive structure through the door, we knew not to lose our shit when the arms did not initially fit. "This is how it happened at The Mock," I told myself. "Remain calm." Sure enough, they eventually found a position that worked.

On its way out of the apartment a year later, however, the couch did not fit through the same doorway. Perhaps its wooden frame had swelled. We ended up having to call Crate and Barrel to drill the couch into bits that we could later re-assemble. The procedure was not expensive, but it took a major toll on both me and Amos. We'd become fairly attached to the thing, which we'd named Blue Balls. (Not only was it was blue, but I refused to have sex on it no matter how heated things got—it simply wasn't wide enough.) Blue Balls has actually never been the same since. It is totally flat in certain areas that were originally bouncy.

Maybe we should have chosen the narrow, burnt orange love seat instead.

After purchasing the Most Hideously Bulbous Down Jacket of All Time, I was, interestingly enough, *100 percent certain* that I needed professional help to learn how to make decisions easier. I asked my mother for a name of a notable cognitive therapist (only one name, otherwise I'd never be able to choose), and I ended up seeing a well-respected, short, boney man, who pointed out that "no one decision alters the rest of your life." Obviously he had never seen *Sliding Doors*, the mediocre movie with Gwyneth Paltrow about how making or not making the subway can change everything.

Ultimately, the guy said nothing I didn't already know intellectually ("We cannot project ahead too much. We can only really focus on the immediate future"), and only solidified my hunch that I was just inherently a nutjob. Plus, he was the CALMEST person ever to walk the earth, so in comparison I felt like a cokehead on speed. Whenever I'd enter his office and say, "Hi!" he'd utter, "Hello..." in the softest, most lulling way possible. I tried to imagine him having an orgasm and concluded that he'd run the risk of being so excessively relaxed afterward that he'd melt into the mattress and have to be scraped off with a cake knife.

Even the therapist's relaxation tapes were unhelpful. They were recordings of his lulling voice telling me to focus my mind on each of my muscles. Squeeze and loosen, he'd say. But I found it impossible to concentrate on my boring muscles. (I have the same problem with yoga. I cannot go into a Downward-Facing Dog without yawning and making a mental list of pros and cons about something, like whether to wait another week for a haircut.)

I've also sampled most medications recommended for indecision, but I'm in constant deliberation about which ones to try and whether they're working. The therapist will say, "Well, have you noticed any difference on this one? Do you feel more strong-minded lately?" I'll reply, "I honestly don't know. One minute I think I'm better because I'll assertively purchase green cotton sheets over blue ones, but the next minute I know for a fact that all I'm going to be thinking about for days is whether I'd be getting more sleep if surrounded by light bluish tones."

Lately, I've been trying to handle my indecision by reminding myself over and over that I am lucky to have options, and that, while regret is super shitty, in the grand scheme there are worse things out there. Watching *ER* helps to put things into perspective. I'll be analyzing which canned soup to heat up later for dinner—the split pea or minestrone—and how the wrong choice could eventually lead to indigestion—and then feel utter relief that I wasn't just impaled on a rusty pole sticking out of the snow.

Now that I think about it, on the off chance that I do encounter a rusty pole in the snow, maybe I should keep wearing the Most Hideously Bulbous Down Jacket of All Time for the added padding—and maybe I should make Amos promise that he'll never fill up on bread and then order a Greek salad.

Or maybe not. I wish I knew.

it's not you, it's me

One rainy Saturday night a couple of years ago when I had a group of friends over and was noticeably low on marijuana, I went to page the drug dealer, but instead accidentally beeped my dentist. I have his number on a similarly colored Post-it by the handle of my refrigerator. It was 1 a.m. and he called back all worried, and I had to pretend there had been a mysterious sudden but fleeting pain in my lower molar.

My dentist is a solid individual. He looks like a handsome version of Ed Begley Jr. from his *St. Elsewhere* days, and his competency knows no bounds. Once, a small air bubble got caught in a pre-crown root canal when I was poking at it with a toothpick outside a Chinese restaurant. I thought my head was going to explode like a sealed plastic container in a microwave. My dentist met me at his office at 4 a.m. to reverse the critical situation and relieve the pressure.

His entire dental gang understands me. The eager assistant, the perky receptionist, the buxom dental hygienist. They get that I'm late for my appointments and that I saturate my teeth with obscene amounts of sugar, but they work *with* these potential hindrances, not against them. They say, "Wendy, if you are going to be late, take the last appointment so you don't back up the whole day." And, "Wendy, if you are going to continue to grind your enamel against cubes of hard caramel, let's get you a prescription fluoride ointment to apply afterward. We know you'll probably never use it and we won't judge you for that, but at least we can all feel good about it being in your possession."

But my dentist and I have unresolved issues. He is the father of my former really good friend, Carly, who, all of a sudden, decided not to be friends with me anymore in sixth grade. Basically, this new girl in school, Rhonda, who was a total bitch, wreaked major social havoc in the class. She convinced my dentist's daughter that two of my friends, Emily and Tracy, and I were highly uncool. And his daughter and I were never friends again. I know it was twenty years ago, but I find it hard to believe that my dentist doesn't remember what happened, and we've never talked about it, and I really feel like it's this unacknowledged *thing* hovering over us as I sit in the chair and he shoots novocaine into my gums.

Plus, nearly everyone who went to my grammar school still goes to him, so I'm bound to run into someone I know at his office. This means that every single time I go to the dentist I have to look really good and have just done something super impressive with my life. Even if I don't run into someone in person, my dentist will surely tell his other patients how I'm doing. At the very least he will tell his daughter, and it is of paramount importance that she thinks I'm the hottest, most thriving person on the planet.

About a year ago, I had to change a dental appointment because I'd gotten my hair cut too short the day before and was unwilling to put myself through any dentist-related scrutiny until it grew back some of its shape. The following day, I overheard a couple of coworkers at my office day job talking about how they loved this one dentist across the street because he was so gosh darn quick. I asked if they had any personal history with the man. They thought that was a really odd question.

I found myself feeling a little jealous of the seemingly simplistic nature of their dental relationships, and came to the conclusion that moving on and cutting the so-called dental cord would be a good move. Not only was the increasing need to impress my dentist and his other patients incapacitating at times, but he had moved to a farther, less convenient location and didn't seem to be free during lunch hours, when I could more easily get away from work. I decided to see the popular dentist across the street for a quick, minor filling.

The guy's office was on a floor entirely dedicated to various dental practices. You could smell tooth decay and hear drills screaming behind every wall. When I opened his door, it banged against the one and only waiting room chair. The receptionist had no visible lips and seemed cold. But when I met the guy, whose large, capped front teeth were blindingly white, I felt incredibly at ease. I didn't care one bit that my eyeliner was smudgy or that I was frustrated at work or that roaches had taken over my apartment. The dentist simply took X-rays and drilled.

That afternoon I sought advice from my coworker Sam, a serial monogamist who's broken a lot of hearts. "I definitely have the right to leave my old dentist, right?" I asked him. "Even after we've shared so much together?"

Sam answered, "Wendy, it is your life, goddammit. You have to go with the new guy if you can look like shit around him. If you had the money to appear glamorous all the time, well, that would be another story. Plus, it is a business relationship. It doesn't matter if he's mad at you. Who cares? Why does everyone have to like you?"

Right. So I formulated a plan for the immediate future: never call the old dentist for an appointment, and if and when I run into any member of the dental gang on the street, say that I've just gotten back temporarily from a prestigious conference in

South Africa for exceedingly successful people in their late twenties.

Soon after, my old dentist's office started leaving me messages on my home answering machine, reminding me about my needed checkup. I couldn't deal with having a potentially awkward conversation, so I didn't call back. Because they were so successful and definitely not in need of my business, I figured they'd eventually forget about me. But one Tuesday morning the perky receptionist called me at the office, and I accidentally picked up because I didn't recognize the number on the caller ID. "Wendy!" she squeaked. "We haven't seen you in *ages*. I'm calling because you need to come in for a checkup. You know you shouldn't go this long."

"Yeah, totally, I know, I've just been so busy . . ."

I couldn't muster up the courage to tell the truth and hoped she'd just take the hint—but then Sam's powerful words came to mind and reminded me that I had every right to go to another dentist. There was another dentist closer to my office!

"I saw another dentist," I said.

Dead silence.

"Because he is so much closer to me, and could see me at one p.m., and work is so busy, and it's really so much more convenient, that's all, and I was going to tell you guys but it's just been so busy, like I just said, and I've been so stressed which is why . . . I needed . . . to see someone else . . . who was closer."

"Oh, I see. Okay. Well, we would have seen you at one p.m. if we knew it meant that much to you. We can still see you at one p.m., ya know."

I couldn't believe this was actually happening. I was obviously *ending things*. I just couldn't do it anymore. Why did they have to be the nicest, most attentive group of people ever? So I pushed the long distance angle. "I'm sorry. It's not just the one p.m. As I said, the other office is *closer*. There's nothing either of us can do about that."

"Well, okay then, I guess. Keep in touch and stay healthy."

The call couldn't have been more gut-wrenching. Still, I felt incredibly relieved that it was done and there was one less messy entanglement in my life to worry about.

UNTIL I GOT AN E-MAIL FROM MY DENTIST. Which literally said something like, "Hi Wendy, it's your dentist. I just heard from my receptionist that you are seeing a new dentist. I don't understand why. We are willing to see you at one p.m. if you really need that time. This other guy can't be that much closer. I know where your office is."

What was I going to say? "Actually, I find it shitty going to you because your daughter made me cry nearly two decades ago, and I think you are telling your other patients about how clogged my pores seem when you loom over me."

So I went back to him.

And we're still seeing one another.

He once met me in the middle of the night to fix an *air bubble* for God's sake. He's the best dentist. There was no way around it.

And he did start conveniently seeing me at 1 p.m.

sticky affairs

I'm fairly certain that getting melted Bazooka all over the High School Boyfriend's roommate's six-hundred-thread-count sheets for the second time in two days—after I'd specifically been told to be extra careful with candy in his bed—was the final straw that put our already frustrating long-distance relationship to an end.

We had been going out for six years and had been living in separate states since going off to college. I was visiting his school in North Carolina for the first time. As usual, I was being especially high-maintenance, and he was being extra patient and supportive. Earlier that week I had convinced myself that I was going deaf because my ears hadn't completely popped after getting off the plane. I had made him wait in line with me for hours at the emergency health center just so an ENT specialist could tell me to hold my nose and blow really hard. My lower intestine also wasn't doing well that month, so he had to borrow a car and drive me to the health food store in town where I bought all sorts of dairy-free products, which I then lugged to all our meals at the university cafeteria. Plus, I had been hit by the car a couple of months earlier, so I was still on crutches with a broken knee at the time. Because he lived in a large frat house, whenever I needed to shower he'd have to get his buddies out of the communal bathroom area, set up my geriatric shower stool, and adjust the water to my desired temperature (just slightly hotter than lukewarm). He normally slept on the top mattress of a bunk bed, but because I couldn't get up and down the ladder with my cumbersome cast, he had made special arrangements for us to sleep in his roommate's bed on the bottom. Which I then somehow COMPLETELY soiled with lackadaisically wrapped and carelessly discarded wads of chewed gum.

Maybe it was a coincidence, but three weeks later we broke up.

For whatever reason, I can't or won't be responsible when it comes to candy. Not only has this caused hiccups in my relationships with men, but it also seems to bother anyone who spends time with me in close quarters. Apparently, every time I take a step forward, I leave behind an amorphous stickiness that "grosses everybody out" and frequently ruins clothes, sofas, rugs, and bedding.

I find the taste of candy to be remarkably calming. The instant it hits my tongue, all anxiety subsides. So I can't eat it just every now and then. I need to have it in the morning, after every meal, while talking on the phone, and right before going to sleep. But I am specific in my tastes. I don't eat chocolate, but I like chocolate-flavored Nips, Tootsie Rolls, and Tootsie Roll Pops. I won't eat black licorice, Sweet Tarts, or Sprees, but I like small cubes of caramel, Bit-O-Honey, and all forms of gummies—worms, bears, cherries, and Coke bottles. I love Twizzlers and Nibs because their taste is subtle, but I am strongly opposed to Red Vines and Twizzlers Pull-n-Peels because their taste is intense right off the bat. Sno-caps SUCK. I like Werther's, but I find it frustrating that the manufacturer refers to them as "Original." (As though there are loads of other kinds of Werther's.) I prefer Bubble Yum bubble gum and Hubba Bubba over Bubblicious because the lack of graininess in the texture of Bubblicious is disappointing. And I refuse to chew sugarless gum. It's a cop-out. I also refuse to chew thin, wimpy stick gum, like Juicy Fruit, Big Red, or Wrigley's Spearmint. People who chew those kinds of gum are looking to keep their jaws busy or to keep from biting their nails or to spice up their breath. I chew gum because I savor and appreciate the taste. And a pack of five is hardly enough. Five is a joke to me. I chew up to fifteen or twenty pieces in one sitting. Each piece usually lasts for about twenty seconds because I feel like I'm wasting my time once the flavor has peaked.

Periodontal issues aside, I'm up to about twenty cavities and eight root canals. But I don't let frequent throbbing nerve pain or postdental recuperation keep me down. If I'm numb on the right, I'll lean my head to the side and dump in Juji Fruits on the left. The cost of frequent dental visits has not been pretty, but ultimately it is a small price to pay for the elation I get from candy on a daily basis. There's just no time to floss and brush my teeth for the recommended two minutes when there's a long brick of Starburst on my nightstand waiting to be consumed.

At first, new friends find my habit endearing. I'll show up to a dinner date holding a pound of gummy worms and they'll say, "Oh, Wendy. You are too funny. You're a hoot!" But as soon as we become closer, my whole candy shtick apparently goes from super sweet to really fucking annoying. The addiction in and of itself is in no way problematic. Things just become hairy when the degree of candy consumption inevitably gets combined with bouts of lethargy and extreme sloppiness.

When I first started working for my former boss as his administrative assistant, he was delighted by my easily accessible candy supply. My cube was just outside his executive corner office, and he'd often stick his head out of his door and bark, "I need some sugar, Wendy. Hand me some Haribo peaches

ASAP." One evening after work we shared a cab to Dylan's Candy Bar, a sugar utopia in midtown Manhattan, and frolicked through the aisles, holding little baggies and scooping out the most exotic samples from the bins. The Juicy Fruit commercial theme song, which echoed from speakers, egged us on, and in appreciation for all my hard assistant work he bought me a do-it-yourself, bubble gum–making machine that took over my life for two solid weeks.

But it wasn't long before my boss started to find cherry-scented film on the corner of his budget reports. Sometimes he'd be sorting through an important file in his office and I'd hear, "WENDEEE!!!!!" He'd emerge holding up two manila folders stuck together by a melted Tootsie Roll. If he ever needed to get office supplies from my desk, he'd stubbornly refuse to open any drawers for fear that he'd witness a monstrous concoction of paper clips, staples, and Skittles residue. He started calling me "dirty girl."

Even now, a year after working there, I still get "thank you" e-mails from him and his new assistant, reporting that they've just found a rotted jelly bean jammed inside a fax machine.

Candy's impact on my relationship with Amos followed a similar trajectory. The night we met, in the computer lab, right before I handed him my sex survey and considered how experienced he might be in the sack, Amos apparently told his friend Jared that he was in the mood for some bubble gum. I had a reputation on campus for giving out candy during parties and classes, so Jared pointed at me and said, "I heard that girl over there is obsessed with candy and likes giving it out. She probably has some on her." Amos came over and I gave him a handful of slightly melting gumballs. The blue and yellow candy shells stained his palm. It was definitely a sign of things to come.

The beginning, honeymoon phase of our romance was one

big, candy-coated montage. He'd surprise me with massive variety packs of Bubble Yum at the movies. We'd share long licorice laces from opposite ends like they were noodles à la *Lady and the Tramp*. Holding hands, we'd saunter from deli to deli looking for rare mini-packs of Lemonheads.

We'd watch the U.S. Open and laugh about how I could use one of those ball girls for my candy habit. How handy would it be if I could drop a Starburst wrapper in the living room, and some girl hiding in the closet could zoom in, grab the wrapper, and zoom out? It would be like mess never happened.

We'd eat Werther's together, and because he'd never sit up straight when popping them in his mouth, I'd worry he'd choke. We'd giggle over the idea of a coroner having to report that there was a "death by Werther's." We'd act it out. (Amos would play the Thorough Detective and I'd be the Coroner):

Thorough Detective: How did this man die?
Coroner: Werther's
Thorough Detective: *Original?*
FIN

I'd also take great pleasure in what we'd refer to as "post-coital candy consumption." Some people light up cigarettes after having an orgasm. I'd lie back on my pillow and pop in a Swedish Fish.

But as time went on, sexual activity had to be postponed because there was candy to finish first. He'd lean over to kiss me and I'd shake my head and mumble, "I've got a couple more lollipops to plow through. And the piece of grape gum in my mouth hasn't even run its course yet. Give it a few more minutes." I could not waste a perfectly flavor-filled piece of gum by aborting the chewing process too soon.

Then, about a year into the relationship, when I was living in Apt. 6C, Amos accidentally sat on a few old, warm red and green Mike and Ikes stuck to one of my dining room chairs. I had noticed them a couple of weeks earlier but hadn't quite mustered up the interest or energy to deal with the mess. He was mildly irritated, but I managed to get most of them off his jeans with a paring knife.

A few months later we took a weekend trip up to his father's house in Connecticut. I was enjoying a large roll of Bubble Tape while we were watching Wallace and Gromit claymation shorts on video in the guesthouse. Because there is no wrapper provided with Bubble Tape, I had piled the twenty or so discarded wads on top of one another inside a Kleenex. When I got up to go to the bathroom, I unknowingly knocked the Kleenex onto the floor, and then accidentally stepped on it when getting back on the couch. The gum broke through the tissue barrier and became entangled in the strands of his stepmother's shag carpet. Amos and I tried to cut it out with scissors but a tough, pink blotch remained. Amos took the blame and apologized, and the family had to purchase a mini-rug to put over the stain.

One of Amos's official boyfriend duties soon became cleaning up after my candy messes—ones I hadn't even realized I'd made. He acted like Penny from *Inspector Gadget*. (Penny was the oblivious detective's responsible niece, who would run around behind Gadget's back and make sure everything went smoothly.) At parties, hastily wrapped chewed pieces of gum and lollipop wrappers would sometimes fall out of a hole in my backpack (I've never liked carrying purses or bags), and Amos would later mention that he'd been clearing my untidy trail like a dog owner picking up the droppings of their overeager untrained puppy.

Right after Amos and I moved in together two years ago, his

new cotton sheets got all fucked-up because three green Dots melted into the elastic of his contour mattress pad. I guess they had rolled out of the box while I'd been zoning out in front of late night *Law & Order: SVU* reruns. Shortly thereafter, he created an official "no candy in the bed" rule. But no candy in the bed—well, yeah. Not that easy.

You'd think I would have learned my lesson after visiting the High School Boyfriend at college—but I had actually blocked out that old bedding/gum incident until a few months ago when Amos woke up with all of the hair on this right forearm plastered to a smear of grape Bubblicious.

He was super mad.

"WENDY! I TOLD YOU NO CANDY IN THE BED! WE HAVE A RULE. I cannot believe this. You . . . Jesus . . . THIS WON'T COME OFF! WAKE UP. NOW! Please help get this off. I'm LATE."

I had never heard Amos that angry before, and I rushed to the bathroom to find cleansing products. I ended up having to cut off most of his forearm hair with a scissor as he shook his head in disgust. Then I blotted him with nail polish remover, which eventually took off the remaining bits. As he stormed out of the house, I started to cry and called his cell.

"Are you going to break up with me?" I sobbed.

"What? What are you talking about?"

"I dunno. I just . . . I just remembered something about visiting my old boyfriend . . ."

"Babe. You're crazy. Calm down. It's just *gum.*"

I thought, *Amos deserves a cleaner, more respectful girlfriend.* In order to make things up to him I immediately left the house and bought him a gift—from our joint bank account. Green, six-hundred-thread-count sheets (the ones I foolishly chose over the light blue ones), which I promised myself I would never ever chew candy in.

The next night, as we were lying side by side reading, he whispered, "What the hell?" There were dark blue prints all over his cheek and shoulder.

I'm sorry, but it's really easy to fall asleep with uncapped felt-tip pens in your hand.

a wedding announcement

I guess I might be sort of "engaged." Last weekend, while I was squeezing a loaf of potato bread at our favorite supermarket, Amos handed me a tinfoil ring he'd made in the kitchen utility aisle. It was well-planned, because the supermarket is one of our favorite places to visit together—when we push the cart and stock up on nonperishables we feel like we're playing "house" full force. He tapped me on the shoulder and whispered, "Marry me." I smothered his prickly semibeard with kisses and clung to his swarthy arm as we sauntered to the paper towel area where we picked up some Bounty.

There was no need for a big to-do because we've known for a while that we've wanted to officially spend the rest of our lives together, and it's just been understood that we would get married soon, and he knows I'm squeamish about elaborate formalities with these sorts of matters. Maybe I'm just rebelling against my grandfather's diamond obsession, but I don't want a typical engagement ring (if any ring at all) and cannot bring myself to say *fiancé* or *engaged*. During the last few years, it has felt increasingly wrong referring to Amos as my "boyfriend" because he is so much more than that, but I simply cannot use those terms. They sound too traditional, or formulaic—or something.

* * *

These feelings might actually stem from my deep loathing of the wedding announcement section of the *New York Times*. The section consists of twenty to thirty pictures of debutante couples, each accompanied by a blurb explaining where they went to college, what jobs they've had, and how they met. Facts about their prestigious families are also included. (The bride's mother is a second cousin of Phil Donohue, the groom's uncle invented the staple remover, the couple's mothers knit shawls for charity.) I don't get my news from the newspaper because it's too unwieldy to hold, but at least once a month I try to pick out and simply scan this section. It's fun to find the two or three announcements in there that contain pictures of *just the woman*. ALL ALONE. With her head tilted slightly toward the right. As if the wedding is all about her. My friend Gail nailed it. She wants to say to these ladies, "Reconsider. I mean . . . if he can't show up for the *photo* . . ." Seriously.

Last Sunday I saw a picture of a nice-looking, freckled couple who were *sharing* a scarf. A scarf was wrapped around BOTH of their necks. 'Nuff said.

Last year, when my dear friend Sumi planned to get engaged, she needed me to check out some potential rings with her at Tiffany one Saturday afternoon. I was wearing my dome-shaped, water-filled, clear plastic glitter ring. As we approached the glass counters, Sumi spotted a platinum ring with a cluster of small diamonds in the center. After taking a closer look, she asked the pristine saleswoman, Brenda (she had a name tag), to take it out of the case. As soon as Sumi slipped it on her finger, Brenda was overcome with enthusiasm. "It's gorgeous on you. It's really a one of a kind piece!"

They both turned to me.

"Um . . . I dunno. It's fine," I said. "I just don't understand, though. They all look the same. How is this one special enough?" Brenda's face turned pale. She leaned in to Sumi and said, "Miss. Of all the friends you might bring to give you ring advice, you choose one who is wearing a snow globe on her finger?" Sumi and I were taken aback. Not only was Brenda witty, but she was also insightful. Sumi replied, "You are so right, Brenda. So right."

In the end, Sumi ended up finding a unique, square-shaped diamond ring that I love, but she quickly learned to take any wedding advice I might offer with a grain of salt.

As her wedding approached, Sumi began visiting various online wedding chat rooms designed for brides to share helpful information about videographers and flower arrangements. Apparently, one time she got overwhelmed by all the logistics and wrote, "Does anyone ever get so sick of all this shite that you wished you could just take a fucking break or just weren't doing it at all and had eloped to Vegas?!" Silence. No one responded. Many of the women were deeply offended and quietly logged off one by one.

These are the women appearing alone in their wedding announcements in the *New York Times*.

Theoretically, I think that announcing one's marriage in a national publication is a wonderful idea. It's awesome that couples want to broadcast their love to the world. But is it always the love that people are proud of? Or is it the status their marriage can bring? I'm never sure because the wedding announcement section doesn't seem to emphasize the *relationship* part of the union. Instead it emphasizes why the couple looks so great together on paper. Not only do their sweaters usually match and their heights correspond, but their backgrounds synch up perfectly. She's a publisher from Rhode Island who went to Haverford. He's a lawyer from California who went to Yale. His family happens to collect Icelandic literature. From the picture you can see that they both have pointy noses and resemble canaries. It's a match made in heaven.

I think what bothers me most is that these announcements help maintain the idea that (a) there is such a thing as a perfect couple and that (b) being a perfectly matched couple is a good thing and not boring as all hell. I admit that I have barely any life experience, so what do I know, but I have encountered good couples and bad couples and can never tell which are the good ones until I spy on them from across the street or sneak behind a grapefruit pile and watch the duo interact in a grocery store. We all know at least one couple that we thought was perfect who ended up getting divorced. And they are usually the one that had the most elaborate wedding.

Or maybe it's that, by making everything seem so perfectly matched and successful and happy-go-lucky, the wedding announcements propagate the fallacy that most people aren't crazy. And one of the only things I'm sure about is that EVERYONE IS SOMEWHAT CRAZY. Correction: really, really two-dimensional people are too boring to be crazy. But everyone who's remotely interesting is crazy. It's just a matter of degree and just a matter of how much they're aware of it. And that's great. But not enough crazy people I encounter know for a fact that most other people are also crazy. They think other people are totally perfect and that's because of things like the wedding section of the *New York Times*.

Marriages would last longer and endure less pressure if things like the marriage announcement section could embrace and celebrate the imperfection of relationships. They shouldn't go and publish all the medication people are taking, but I want to know about the couple that was "on a break" and then got back together after they sowed wild oats. The ones who have only known each other for a month but can't afford living apart in Manhattan, and don't believe in living together before marriage. The ones who have a diseased rat problem in their basement.

But maybe that's just me.

And maybe Amos and I should submit a picture of just Amos to the *New York Times*.

His might be the first lone guy picture ever submitted.

I sort of like that idea.

stranger bonding

A few years ago, while running weekend errands on Lexington Avenue, I was lured into a physically tiny yet massively tacky store called Infinity, which targets teens and women in midlife crises. I was only having a quarter-life crisis, but was equally susceptible to the allure of the loud turquoise beaded cardigan showcased in the window. Upon entering, I saw a tan woman in her mid-forties with an intense bowl cut struggling to undo the button on a pair of stretch, acid-washed jeans that had adhered themselves to her body. Ripples upon ripples of stomach poured over the waistline. She hobbled back and forth outside her dressing room mumbling, "Uh, someone, girls . . . one of you girls . . . I'd like to buy these but I can't get them off . . . can someone help me, please?"

One of the younger clerks came over and eagerly offered assistance. "Suck in and I'll pull from this end."

I watched in anticipation while pretending to peruse the tank tops, forgetting all about the turquoise beady bait that had originally brought me inside. While the woman sucked, the girl got down on her knees, awkwardly grasped the fabric and leaned backward, eventually losing her grip and falling into a soft pile of tie-dyed leggings. The cashier grabbed a small mic by the counter and paged the manager. "Diane. Diane. Can you come out from the stock room for a moment? We have a small situation here." Diane emerged holding a calculator and clipboard and politely attended to the crisis. "How can I help you, ma'am?"

"I can't get these pants . . . off . . . I just . . . my stomach . . . the button won't . . . go . . ."

Perhaps this was an everyday occurrence at Infinity because Diane matter-of-factly marched away and returned with a handy set of pliers from the back room.

The customer stood on a small wooden stool holding up her shirt as the manager crouched and operated on the latch. The staff huddled around offering encouragement. "Almost there . . . almost . . . YES . . . oooo . . . close." I heard someone mutter, "I mean, if you got in them, you must be able to get out of them . . ." But this lady defied science.

Despite the fact that she had found a way to squeeze the pants on, there was no seemingly plausible way of getting them off without scissors, and I guess because she was going to have to pay for them regardless, the woman then gave up and just bought the jeans on her body. In order to ring her up, they had to lower the pricing gun from the cash register onto the tag peeking out behind her protruding butt crack. During the credit card transaction, she actually seemed perfectly psyched with her purchase. As if she had come to terms with the inconvenience and had figured, *Well, I'll just wear them out dancing tonight and look so piping hot that it will be worth it.* I really wonder if she decided to go out on the town that night to get the most out of the pants until she'd have to cut them to shreds before going to bed.

Now, almost everything about this Infinity incident was fantastic, but it would have been true utter perfection had there been a stranger at the store to connect with. Unfortunately, the two other shoppers were fourteen years old, and they had been digging through a bin of rhinestone leather belts and had missed the entire thing.

I just *relish* the act of bonding with strangers. There is something almost romantic about people who don't know one another, who will never know one another, sharing such a special, pleasant, and fleeting thing as a funny moment. But for this type of bonding to occur, there really needs to be mutual, active interest from all parties. Otherwise, it just sucks. Like once, I was walking through Central Park when I saw a wobbly toddler wearing flared green pants. His legs were so short that the flare took up most of the pant. He looked like he was wearing triangles. He was learning to walk, but afraid to lift one of his feet, so he only went in a circle. His tall, unshaven father turned to me before carrying him away, shrugged, and said, "He likes to pivot."

The whole scenario was pretty damn cute.

I looked at a blond woman standing nearby who had also witnessed the scene and hoped we would bond about it all. But she only smiled mildly as if to say, "That's nice but I'm late for a hair appointment and I don't know you." It wasn't a matter of *opinion*: the father's comment was witty and the overall scene with the triangular pants and the circular motion was, at the very least, amusing. I didn't expect us to launch into full-on girly hysterics, but a little more acknowledgment on her part would have been nice. I felt a little rejected.

Actually, unreciprocated bonding like this makes reciprocated bonding that much more rewarding. Once, when I was on a crowded crosstown bus on my way to high school, a random female voice yelped, "My shoe!" and a black pump went flying across people's heads toward the rear. It was unclear if it made a smooth landing so there was general concern in the air. I made eye contact with a businessman in his fifties sitting across the way. We both smirked and rolled our eyes, implying, *New York is wacky sometimes, ain't it?* The flying of the shoe itself wasn't that big of a deal, but the connection I shared with the man (someone I would never befriend under normal circumstances) was deeply fulfilling because we were equally invested.

My most rewarding episode of Stranger Bonding to date transpired at a wedding in New York City last summer. An acquaintance from my sociology class in college, who I hadn't spoken to since second semester *sophomore year*, had sent me a wedding invitation. We had no friends in common, so I didn't know anyone going. I wasn't even allowed to bring a date. But because I was flattered that she had thought of me, and I didn't have any other plans, I felt obligated to attend.

The reception was pretty big—250 guests, maybe—and took place in SoHo at a long dining hall smothered in lilacs. A gargantuan chandelier, poised to rain down daggers of glass at any moment, swayed high above our heads. I was seated at Table 31, with eleven people I had never met before—six men and five women of varying ages. (Something about getting a seat assignment at a large wedding for a couple you barely know is frighteningly similar to serving on jury duty. You show up partly out of obligation and partly out of curiosity, get placed with a random sampling of society, are forced to watch a performance— sometimes boring, sometimes emotional—and then analyze the potential outcome as a group.) After an uninteresting discussion about whether it was wiser to order pancetta-wrapped filet mignon or salmon in a light lemon-dill sauce, we politely expressed our contrived faith in the couple's success. (I, at least, had nagging doubts. I obviously wished them well, but the mere fact that Jane and Rob had considered me enough of a dear friend to be a part of this special day suggested a skewed understanding of human relationships in general and a probable separation within the year.)

Anyway, at Table 31 there was a blond guy with great dimples, maybe twenty-three years old, sitting next to a shorter, younger-looking, dirty blond guy with equally Nordic coloring. They had the type of rosy cheeks people get after being out in the snow for an extended period of time, and I hoped they modeled for Patagonia. After we placed our orders and received our small garden salads, I saw that the two had started to snuggle and kiss. I was pleased because they made an excruciatingly gorgeous couple. But within minutes, the hugging and kissing devolved into an extreme public display of affection. They were completely entwined, one leg over the other's lap. They were tickling one another's neck and armpits with arugula. At one point the dimple guy licked vinaigrette dressing off the other guy's *palm*. They kept connecting the top of their foreheads and closing their eyes as if to momentarily channel souls.

Everyone at the table desperately tried to chat and eat normally but it was impossible to focus on anything other than the PDA. In an attempt to break the madness, a heroic woman in her forties seated next to me turned to them and said, "So, how do you guys know Rob and Jane?"

"Cousins," said the dimple guy.

"Oh, how nice. So you are the cousin?"

"*We* are the cousins."

I almost choked on my flowered carrot.

Clarification was desperately needed, so I took it upon myself to add, "So that makes you guys *also* cousins? To *each other*?"

"No, no . . ." said the other guy.

Everyone let out a massive sigh of relief. You could hear the release of tension over the clinking of silverware.

"We're twins," he continued. "*We* are Jane's cousins."

I thought, *It doesn't get better than this*. But then it did. Because as I looked around at the strangers at Table 31, I felt intense

camaraderie. Suddenly it was as if we had spent a month together on a deserted island, sharing our life stories over stunning bonfires and pitching in to build an astounding bamboo
raft.

When the woman next to me excused herself, it was understood that the rest of us would follow. We headed toward the
bathrooms and formed a huddle. Between hysterical laughter,
we pondered the important questions. "What the fuck?" "Are
they bluffing?" "Are we on *Candid Camera*?" "Does the family
know?"

I marched back into the reception and headed straight to the
main table where the bride and groom were formally picking at
their meal. After congratulating them again on the lovely deco-
rations, I added, "I love my table too. Your cousins over there are
adorable. They're your cousins, right?"

The bride responded, "Yes. The twins are great. Aren't they
soooo hot? So glad you like everyone."

"Right. Later."

I ran back to the bathroom and confirmed that the blonds
were indeed relatives of the bridal party *and* relatives of one another.

Our plan was to return to the table, stare, and hope that one
of us would think of a probing yet nonjudgmental-sounding
question. Just as we reentered the reception hall, the DJ started
blaring Prince, and a ferocious mob of bridesmaids hit the
dance floor in red heels. Unable to dodge the stampede, my
right pinky toe got crushed by a stiletto and soon swelled to the
size of a quarter. But the adrenalin from all the bonding was so
powerful that I barely felt the pain.

As I limped back to the table with the help of my team, the
cousins were nowhere in sight. When it was clear that the mysterious duo had left the wedding altogether (their jackets were

gone and plates taken away), we nibbled at our food while analyzing the absurdity of it all. After the lemon cake was cleared, it was difficult to say goodbye.

"Well, nice meeting you guys," I said. "Great sharing those moments with ya."

Even though we had barely exchanged *names*, we then spent thirty minutes writing our e-mail addresses on "Rob and Jane" embossed napkins. It was obvious that no one planned to actually keep in touch, but it was necessary to go through the motions because, after watching ridiculously good-looking male twins passionately make out, we had become a tightly knit family.

I'd like to think that wherever they are, whatever they're doing, the other members of Table 31 also occasionally remember our time together. I trust that, although we will never speak again, our bond continues to be just as strong as it was that humid day in June.

mom's big break

So Mom has just come around to accepting that I won't be pursuing business, law, or dermatology.

She's finally let go of her firm belief that if you are going to pursue a creative hobby, it should really be kept on the side like a spicy salad dressing or fattening mayonnaise. Basically, a few months ago, when I performed a one-woman show in Los Angeles about my family, an NBC executive told the producer, "Yeah, Wendy was great, but, well, I'm very interested in her *mother*." (I had shown some home movies with her talking slooowly and wearing multiple layers of shoulder pads.) He wanted to set up a meeting with her and some TV casting directors in New York. Pronto. I believe he was considering her for a reality show in development about a pack of feisty Jewish mothers raging around town giving sex advice to singles. Like *Queer Eye for the Straight Guy,* but with moms.

I was so elated that I forgot about the three-hour time difference to New York and called her from my cell phone.

"Mom! NBC wants you! You have to audition, Mom—you have to, you have to!"

"Wha? It's one a.m., dear. Is everything okay?"

"You are going to be a star, Mom. Someone from NBC wants you for a new part on a TV show!"

"Oh? But . . . I . . . I'm not formally trained. I did study acting in high school. Though—"

"They just want you to be yourself. You're funny as yourself."

"Myself? Oh. Oooh. Well how soon do they need to meet . . . I mean, Wendy, I have horribly dark roots right now, and I'll need a manicure."

"I'll figure it out and put someone in touch with you soon."

"Okay. Sure. Any idea how soon they'll call? I mean, it would be good to know, just, well because . . . HOW SOON??"

"I dunno, Ma, I'll have my agent call you this week."

Mom called me right after her audition was scheduled. "So, I'm all set to go in on Tuesday morning. I'm taking off part of the afternoon on Monday to mentally prepare and see a hair stylist. I've called a car service to pick me up an hour before. You can't depend on getting a cab at that hour."

She also called me the moment she got out of the audition. "It went well, and they laughed, but maybe they do that with everyone? I talked about sex among young people today and how the Internet is a good way to couple up. You know, JDate or Nerve.com. I seemed hip. But I think my chin comes across too low on camera, and the woman told me to talk faster a couple of times. She says I drag out my words. When will we know?"

I told her we'd just have to wait.

Hours later she called my agent in a panic. "Listen—I almost forgot—you should really let the producers know something veeery important. In late February, I will *not* be available. I have jury duty."

Then she called back to clarify, "And . . . can I call you *my agent*? Is this official?" She was reassured. She had representation in the biz.

One morning a couple of weeks later my mom called me to share the latest update. "Soooo . . . dear, just want you to know. I didn't get the part. But I feel fine about it. I mean, it turns out . . . they went in *another direction.*"

She admitted that she'd gotten pretty caught up in the process, though, and well, couldn't be more thrilled that I was pursuing artistic dreams . . . as long as I kept in touch with all my psychology professors from college. (I would need to use them as references for medical school if I ever tried to become a dermatologist. You know, as a backup plan.) A month later, she gathered a bunch of friends together and somehow produced an Off Off Broadway musical called *Miami Beach Monsters*. It was about Frankenstein, his bride, Wolfman, and Dracula retiring to a rental house in Florida. It had a short, two-month run in a small theater in Chelsea.

My mom also suggested that we develop a mother/daughter bit to take on the road. "Can you pull some strings and get us a gig at The Funny Bone in Long Island? I hear it's a great venue. With great sound quality."

Currently my mother has been brainstorming and pitching jokes I should use in my writing. Ironically, they are usually about the career paths I abandoned.

"Wendaay, I've been thinking. Why don't you do a joke about all the red tape these days? How about you say, 'to be a doctor . . .' Now, you'll need to have a pause there because that is the entrée to the punch line. So you'll say, 'to be a *doctor* . . . with all the paperwork for all the HMOs . . . you need to be a *lawyer*!' HA! Wow. Funny stuff. So you'll use that, right? You'll use that in the book? I want to contribute to the book."

"Mom, you're the best. Don't worry. I'll make sure that joke makes it in somehow."

gary

One Thursday afternoon, the summer after I graduated from college, while Amos and I were exhaling smoke from a tall glass bong in my bedroom, my mother meandered by while pinching her nostrils together in disgust. "Hmmph. Just like *Gary*," she moaned.

"What?" I asked. She proceeded to tell me that Gary, my father, had smoked too much pot as an adult and that the smell had driven her batty.

At the time I wasn't curious enough about my father to push the issue. I thought it was cool that he'd been a stoner and was content to leave it at that. It's not that I didn't care or ever think about my father's death. It was incredibly sad that a man's life was cut short and that my mother and grandparents had endured a severe loss. I just, well, never felt very personally affected. How could I miss something I never had?

This was how it was until a few years ago, when I started working for an older, married man in his mid-thirties—my first male boss. (This was the same man whose budget reports I would soil with candy residue.) He was an important vice president and I was his administrative assistant with little interest in and thus no short-term memory for anything administrative-related. Even if I jotted one of his requests down on a Post-it, my handwriting was often so bad that I'd be unable to read my own reminders. I didn't have the patience for filing, so important documents were mixed in with lunch menus and fax cover sheets, and I'd rarely be able to find whatever he needed urgently. And in addition to leaving sticky sugar trails everywhere, sometimes I got so hungry at my claustrophobic desk that I'd recklessly dig into a garden salad and spill bright orange French dressing on the message pads.

In order to make myself feel like a useful employee who was worthy of a salary, I tried doing what I thought I might do better than administrative assistance: breaking up the monotony of office life. Once, when my boss was on an important conference call with China, I popped in to offer him a Slim Jim that I'd found by the watercooler. "You know who you remind me of?" he asked. "You remind me of that small, animated paper clip on Microsoft Word. You bounce around and try to be helpful . . . but just end up being kinda annoying." I took this as a compliment.

Sometimes when he was in the bathroom, I'd go into his desk drawer and sprinkle pinch-fulls of exceptionally prissy pink glitter from my eye shadow collection all over his presentation materials. Once, early on, when he was doing an on-camera interview about market trends, the reporter had to stop and say, "Uh, people, we're gonna have to shoot that again. Sir? I . . . I think you have a sparkle . . ." My boss looked up at the ceiling, shook his fist in the air, and bellowed, "WENDEEE!" in a Ralph Kramden manner.

Later that afternoon he called me to his big oak desk.

"Wendy, I'm serious. I found glitter on my *deodorant*. Enough."

"Look," I said. "I'm never gonna be one of those typical, boring, 'legible handwriting,' 'organized,' people. So if that's what you really want in an assistant, then I think I should probably leave."

Luckily, he answered, "Calm down. Jesus. I don't want you to *leave*. I couldn't survive all this crap without you. You make me happy. Last Tuesday, you stuck a *gold star* on my paycheck."

And for the first time as his assistant, I felt understood, truly appreciated, and accomplished. I had always been properly thanked for specific tasks, but I'd never been particularly praised. I had never heard a resounding "Great job!" Mainly because I never did a great job. But even if I had, it's nearly impossible to do a *great* job coordinating a conference call. You either coordinate the call or you don't. You can't put in tons of extra hours and coordinate the shit out of it. Because I was supposed to make everything go smoothly, my work only got noticed when something went wrong. But this man noted my stupid pranks and actually liked me for them. He didn't seem to take his job too seriously, and there's nothing worse than corporate people who act like they're in the ER.

The next day my boss's boss visited our office and hollered to her assistant, "In five minutes you need to start rolling some calls, okay?" (This is the practice whereby the assistant makes a call ahead of time and then connects her boss when the needed person is on the phone.) Within two seconds my boss poked his head out of his office and, with the same urgency, muttered, "Wendy, in five minutes you need to start rolling some joints, okay?"

I was in good hands.

I then officially decided to ignore all formal responsibilities and concentrate solely on getting my boss to holler my name in that wonderfully annoyed but slightly amused Ralph Kramden manner whenever I did something he found simultaneously charming and retarded.

At one point, he had to attend a formal business conference in Miami. A few weeks beforehand, the business conference people called and requested a picture of him to put on the name tag that he would have to wear to all the important seminars and meetings. I sent them a nice matte photo of Bert (of Bert and Ernie/*Sesame Street* fame) in a red business suit. I heard from his colleague that he wore the pass and hollered my name the entire week.

My boss also enjoyed my Street Jets fixation. Street Jets are Inspector Gadget–like sneakers that, with a touch of a button, turn into roller skates. I saw a commercial for them one Sunday afternoon during an *E! True Hollywood Story* and called the toll-free number. Their largest children's size was equivalent to an adult size five, and they fit me perfectly. Wearing them in the office was especially neat. Boss needs some tape? I'd zoom across the hall like a fairly successful, highly coordinated actress in *Starlight Express*.

In return for my antics, my boss let me get away with anything. I basically had my own, openly acknowledged company *within* the company. I'd begun to focus more and more on a performing career, and took full advantage of office supplies and FedEx and messenger accounts. One Monday I told him I was going downstairs to get some manila envelopes and he said, "Really. When was the last time I sent anything out?"

"Um . . . never?"

"Ah. 'Wendy, Inc.' is low on envelopes?"

I took a deep breath and admitted, "Yeah, we're pretty low right now."

Now, I'm not into stealing or anything. I shoplifted *once* in twelfth grade when I really wanted a spread on my bagel, but didn't have any money on me, and plucked a tub of cream cheese from the nearby supermarket. It was nice to not have to eat the bread dry, but the guilt was too much to bear and I never did anything like it again. (I know this isn't a good reason, but I also felt like it was okay to take cream cheese from this particular establishment because, like many corporate offices, it seemed to take itself too seriously. Its name, Gristedes 2000, flashed in gaudy green and blue colors in every aisle. This was in the mid-nineties so 2000 was supposed to seem futuristic. Why the supermarket felt the need to go out of its way to market itself all overly slick and tacky is beyond me. It's not like they had voice sensor checkouts with automatic bagging technology or their food was organically grown in a spaceship. And they were clearly not thinking long term. Now it's 2006, and Gristedes 2000 is actually still up and running. The aura of the place feels brutally depressing. It needs to stick around for another fifty years, so it becomes retro and therefore cool again.)

Anyway, I quickly learned that if you work for a business owned by a big rich monopoly and you are not an exceptionally rule-abiding citizen, you often "borrow" things from your workplace, so much so that you start to believe your own lies. Like once, my mother asked to wear a purple pashmina-wool shawl that she had given me for my birthday. I was more than happy to give it back to her—I would never use a shawl—but it was a Friday and she needed it that night before going to a wedding the next day, so I ordered a messenger from work and had it brought to her house across town. A couple of weeks later I got a small slip of paper delivered to my cube. It was an invoice asking me to pay the company forty dollars for that messenger. I called HR.

"Hi, excuse me, but I just got a notice saying I have to pay for a messenger?"

"Yes, well in the records it says that your package was going to a Spero. Your last name is Spero, and if you send items to family members, that is obviously considered personal and the company won't pay."

I was stunned. I mean, I *could have* sent something work-related to my mother's house for me to look at over the weekend. Yes, okay, maybe I *didn't* send something work-related, but that was beside the point. I *could have*. How dare they doubt me.

I remained poised and responded coolly, "But I had files sent to my mother's house because I stayed there all weekend. I organized the files. It was completely work related."

"Oh. Really?"

"Yes."

At this point, I had taken such a stand that I believed my own story. I literally created a memory of working over the weekend and actually thought, *This is so ridiculous because those files took five hours to organize.*

The woman said, "Oh, we're so sorry. Don't worry about the payment, then. Sorry for the mix-up."

I was genuinely outraged and marched into my boss's office to commiserate. He was totally with me and yelled, "You *could have* been sending files or something to your mom's house! How dare they question it!"

"I KNOW! I basically almost organized files at her house!"

We both sighed in disbelief.

Amos once experienced a slightly similar version of this phenomenon when he was working at an Internet start-up doing computer programming. To carry out part of his job, he was using one of their old laptops at home. When the business got bought by a big monster company, Amos, along with every other employee, was laid off and asked to return all equipment. But Amos convinced himself that the computer was his to keep because he was out of a job and needed a computer, and the monster company could clearly afford billions of new high-tech models. When an executive called Amos at home to remind him to bring it in, he replied, "Actually, it doesn't work correctly and I don't think you'd even want it."

"Oh, it's okay," the man said. "We could probably fix it."

"Really, it's unfixable."

"We don't care. We definitely could use it anyway."

"Actually the screen is completely bashed in," Amos lied.

"The screen bashed in? Hmm. Well, I still need to see it. Please bring it by tomorrow at three p.m. Thanks!"

Amos hit rock bottom as he sat in his bedroom and ferociously attacked a perfectly good computer with a screwdriver. The tool wouldn't tear through the thick screen so he convinced me to bring over one of the old, insanely sharp utensils from my knife collection. After hours of hard labor, Amos successfully demolished the machine and shamefully returned it to its rightful owner. When the man took the machine from Amos and saw how bad it looked, he said, "Yeah, you're right. It's really busted. I'm so sorry I made you take the trip out here."

For days all Amos could do was complain about how shitty it was that the guy hadn't believed him. He kept repeating, "I told him it was useless. I mean, the screen was completely bashed in!"

When I told my boss this computer story, he totally understood Amos's pain, and it strengthened our resolve to become a dynamic duo united against corporate America. He began taking me to lunches, where we'd gab about our straight-edged coworkers and he'd give me fatherly advice about housing issues and finances.

We took exceptional pleasure in the ludicrousness of business e-mails. Our internal e-mail system was configured in such a way that personal e-mails were often accidentally sent to hundreds of people. A little icon with the company-wide address was frighteningly close to the "to" line of a new mail message, so if you were at all jittery your mouse could easily stray into dangerous territory. Almost every day a note saying something like, "Yeah, Sheila's a cow" would pop into your in-box. You'd think, *Sheila? Vice President Sheila? Who's Rob? Wait, Rob is Sheila's new assistant. Oooo.*

These embarrassing incidents were exacerbated when the person attempted to reverse his or her actions. There was no way to get the server to suck the letter back. If you asked the computer to undo a sent item, another memo saying something like, "PLEASE DO NOT PAY ATTENTION TO THE PREVIOUS MESSAGE SENT OUT BY ROB" would automatically go out to the same recipients. This would, of course, further highlight the person's fatal mistake.

My boss and I kept a formal tally of these e-mails. He actually asked that I print them out and file them in an important "folder of shame." Even though I didn't believe in filing, I was happy to make an exception in this case. I even alphabetized them by last name. Anything to impress this increasingly paternal figure in my life.

One night my boss invited me to an after-work party at an obscure bar in the East Village. I was so psyched that he had asked, and so psyched to hang out with him totally outside the office. There was a little antique phone booth in the corner of the bar, and we decided it would be neat to get high in it. (We had discovered that pot was a mutual interest of ours early on, after bonding over having to take the company's ridiculous drug test. But we'd never actually gotten stoned together.) As we walked over we both noticed that, randomly, Hugh Grant was leaning on the door. My boss tapped Hugh on the shoulder and asked, "Hey. We're gonna do drugs in there. Wanna come?" Hugh looked at us in his overdone baffled Englishman way and muttered, "Okay."

The three of us tried to squeeze in, but there was clearly only enough space for two. I turned to my boss and yelled, "GET OUT!"

"No. I'm staying," he said. "I'm not gonna let anything 'happen' here. I'm gonna cock-block Hugh Grant."

"No you're *not*," I replied, pushing him out of the way.

So I'm standing there with Hugh Grant, who I really think had some form of makeup on his face, and as I passed the joint I looked past him, past the pane doors of the booth, and saw my boss. Waving. Giving me a thumbs-up.

Hugh started coughing in an embarrassing manner and yelped, "This grass is horrid! You're poisoning me!" and stormed out.

My boss rushed in, begging for details.

I announced: "He's an idiot."

We high-fived and collapsed into the booth, hysterically laughing. Later, after eating late-night fries at a nearby diner, he put me in a taxi and insisted on giving me fare for the cab ride home.

In bed that night, I tried to identify what had been so darn exhilarating about the evening. Oddly it wasn't Hugh Grant. Or even Hugh Grant's beige facial foundation. The adventure seemed somehow different from a fun night out with a friend, but it definitely was not romantic either. I concluded that I felt like a little kid who had just gone on a fishing trip with her cool dad.

A few months later, my boss had an actual kid. So, in addition to feeling more and more entrenched in a bizarre workplace father-daughter dynamic, I got to witness a stoner, fratty, party-going, executive transform into a mushy parent. When his son was first born, he said, "Yeah, it's cool, I really love it, ya know, and it's cute . . . but, I feel weird kissing it, ya know . . . cause it's a *guy*." (He denies it now, but he really said this.)

But as weeks went by, my boss became completely invested. I once saw him kiss the boy on the lips for five minutes. Eventually, a year or so later, he'd get him on speakerphone at the end of every workday and the toddler would say, "Okay, Dad. I love you, bye . . . Let's have lunch. Have your people call my people." My boss would program him for hours to say things like that.

I started to wonder if my father would have been into me in the same way. My father was a therapist, so maybe he would have called me every day from *his* office and had me say something like, "Okay, Dad. I love you, bye . . . I'm afraid we're out of time. See you next week."

Soon, I became obsessed with my boss's kid. I wasn't a stalker (I don't think), but I'd find myself in the middle of a Saturday night party pondering the density of his adorable fleshy cheeks. When he smiled, it was clear he was painfully struggling to lift the corners of his mouth because of the massive weight of the sides of his face.

When he got a little older, the boy started calling the office regularly. I'd answer the phone and pathetically try to talk to him for as long as possible, just so I could imagine his cheeks wobbling up and down as he spoke. I'd inevitably turn into one of those annoying adults I used to despise, and coo, "What did you eat for lunch today?"

"Pasta," he'd answer.

"Do you like pasta?"

"Yeah."

"Do you like the *shapes* of pasta?"

"Yeah."

"Did you help make the pasta?"

"Yeah."

"Maybe we can make pasta together sometime!"

"Is my dad there?"

"Uh, sorry, hold on."

I thought, *If I'm feeling this utterly invested in my boss's kid, how insane must it be to be an actual parent?*

And then one evening I begged my boss to stop by Apt. 6C after he finished his late work dinner right across the street. (I know it seems weird to have your boss come to your house, but I was eager to have him meet Puddle.)

As soon as he made it up the stairs and sat on the couch for a minute to catch his breath, I brought him into my room to show him the finger puppets. He started looking at the family pictures on my compact wooden nightstand. On the lower hidden shelf was a small, framed picture of me and Gary in a cute embrace. My boss turned to me and asked, "Wendy . . . why is this picture so hidden? I mean . . . this photo is important. It should be on a higher shelf. On the middle shelf or the top shelf." He was noticeably disturbed for the man in the photo. At that moment, for the first time ever, really, I felt sad for a cool stoner dad whose child didn't remember him or have an interest in finding out about him. And I felt guilty for calling him Gary. I imagined him somehow hearing me call him by a proper name and being hurt.

I concluded that if, God forbid, anything bad ever happened to my boss, it would be a colossal shame for his son to never know him or all the great things about him. And a "colossal shame" was an understatement.

Maybe because I felt self-conscious asking my mother too many questions directly, or maybe because I was scared I'd upset her if I pried too much into their life together, I casually asked her to make a list of Gary's friends. People I could maybe try to get in touch with. She compiled a list . . . a list of *two* names. Grammar school, high school, college, medical school. *Two* names. Okay then.

I called the first one up. A guy by the name of Paul Lerner, someone Gary had apparently known since childhood. We met for lunch at a dark Italian restaurant in midtown. There were little red lamps at each table and there was dark red paint on the walls. It felt like there was going to be a bullfight at any moment. It was not the quaint daytime dining café that might suit a casual reunion with your dead father's friend.

After we had the initial confusing blind-datish, "Hi . . . are . . . you Paul? Yes, I'm Wendy" banter, we sat down under the red radiance and he said, "So, Wendy. I guess you want to know about your father. Well, we were close, actually . . . he was my best buddy . . . until we were about . . . well . . . I'd say maybe . . . six or seven. And then we pretty much lost touch after that."

Long pause.

I waited for more. But no, that was it. That was all he had.

And it turned out that right before we met he had ordered extra bread, soup, salad, calamari, pasta, AND a large chicken dish. We were about to embark on a five-course meal for no reason whatsoever.

He did remember one important thing. Apparently, Gary was good at "tag."

Good to know.

But right about when the soup arrived, he took out a piece of paper from his briefcase and explained, "I have something for you. This belonged to your father. Your grandfather gave it to me at his funeral and . . . I want you to have it."

"Really, are you—are you sure?"

"Yes. It's yours."

He handed me a laminated sheet of yellowy old loose-leaf paper. Suddenly there was an artifact—an actual thing that had been written by my father—in my hand. I eagerly went to read it. But then he buried his face in his hands and sighed, "I lost my job last week . . ."

"Oh, wha . . . I'm so sorry . . . um . . . I guess . . . I'll just . . . put this away."

And for *two hours* he told me about all his problems with his boss and coworkers. I felt for him, I did, but the whole time I had the key to my father's *existence* within reach.

FINALLY, when the chicken dish had been consumed and we had analyzed every aspect of his layoff, I happily said good-bye to Paul Lerner. I rushed out of the dark redness and took out the document. My eyes slowly adjusted to the daylight. I saw that it said "By Gary Spero" up at the top next to "Health Class." I guessed that this was something my father wrote in school.

I read the first line: "Paul Lerner wears thin-rimmed glasses." I scanned down and slowly realized that the entire paper was *about* Paul Lerner. "Paul uses food to ease his pain." Yes, he does. "Paul is bad at long-term friendships." "Paul has an unnaturally close relationship with his sister."

Uh, this was all *bad stuff* about Paul Lerner.

So, (a) *how* inappropriate was it of my grandfather to give him this at all?! Let alone AT the funeral. "Here. Here is a paper about *all* your shortcomings—including your unnaturally close relationship with your sister—written by my dead son." And (b) I learned nothing from the entire encounter about Gary, but did learn an *enormous* amount about Paul Lerner.

I called the other guy on the list who I knew was a college buddy of Gary's. He lived in Canada, so there was no chance of a long, drawn-out discussion about job security over endless orders of chicken cutlets in an inappropriately dark red bistro. He said that Gary was known for being jokey, quirky, hammy, and unconventional. But when I asked for specific examples, he answered, "Yeah, to be honest, well, ya know, I wasted a lot of brain cells . . . I don't remember a lot from college . . . so well, you know."

Okay. Can I just say something?

If any of my friends have a baby—maybe some of you reading this now—if any of *you* guys have a baby and then you die, *I* will befriend the baby. I will keep in touch with the baby. I will tell the baby all about you and how much you loved the baby. *I* will do that for you. That is the kind of person I am.

But *Gary* apparently didn't know anyone. Mom says that men don't keep in touch the way women do. I still don't know if I buy that, but regardless, I hit a bit of a dead end. But then my mom hunted through my grandfather's old video collection and found Super 8 film footage of Gary and me. She suggested I take it to a video place and have it converted to VHS.

So I did.

And I sat at home eating Twizzlers while watching grainy close-up seventies film footage of a chubby, hairy, bearded man holding a baby and repeating, "Wendy. Helloooo. Speak to me, Wendy. Say something, sweetie."

It was strange to hear him say my name.

Then he picked up the camera and filmed my mother bouncing me and whispering, "Wendy. Wave to Daddy."

For the first time I saw my family as a threesome and not as a twosome. And heard my mom say the word "daddy."

And then my mom gave me his diary.

He had kept it during college. I came across this passage: "It scares me to no end that my time here is so short. Life is just too short." Weird.

I read on, desperately trying to decode his boyish cursive. I saw that it also said, *very* clearly: "Jesus, I have masturbated at least a thousand times in the past two years if not more."

And then there were literally ten pages about masturbating. He worried his penis was getting too overworked; he worried he'd run out of sperm.

I'm not sure that's exactly how Gary would have wanted to be remembered by his daughter.

But I really like these passages. They're brilliant. Especially because in the home video Gary looked an awful lot like the porn star Ron Jeremy.

From what I've gathered so far, it seems that my father was affectionate, funny, unconventional, pot smoking, and horny. The type of guy who might have appreciated glitter on his presentation materials. Who might have collected embarrassing business e-mails. Who might have joked with someone about cock-blocking Hugh Grant. Who might have taken great pleasure in a microcosmos.

Now I know where that comes from.

mini driver

Despite my attachment to the comforting nightlight that is New York City, the coziness of my mother, and the support of my friends, Amos and I did recently move to Los Angeles, to a suburb in West Hollywood. It's a long story. It's fine. It's totally temporary. Actually, the dewy lawns smell really nice. I've got a decent pink strip of sunburn across my nose, and I'm actually getting a major kick out of the garbage disposal and all the buying-in-bulk. Earlier tonight Amos and I purchased a ten-pack of generic antiseptic wipes from Costco and I couldn't have been happier about it. Plus, there's far more room here for Joyce and the rest of my beloved stuffed animals to flourish.

But there is one L.A. thing that I wasn't prepared for, and it is the one thing in the world that truly feels like the antithesis to everything I've ever known.

Driving.

I do not know how to drive, and I don't think I'll ever know how to drive, and those who think otherwise have no real grasp on reality. They say to me, "Wendy, driving is just like riding a bike! You'll suddenly get it and won't have to think about it anymore." This is entirely unhelpful because I've never ridden a bike and I know I could never learn. They also say to me, "Wendy, really dumb people are driving around in those cars out there. If most really dumb people in the world can drive, *you* can drive." This is also entirely unhelpful because in my gut I know that in a specific, indescribable way I am actually dumber than most of the dumb people out there.

Perhaps it's my Manhattan upbringing, but I can't even imagine myself driving on a theoretical level. I'm only barely able grasp the notion of my peers driving. I still see driving as an exceptionally mature activity only to be performed by my mom's friends who live in the country. Every time I get in a car with someone my age, for a split second I cannot help but think, *Uh, shouldn't there be a grown-up present?*

Navigating through faded, dotted, curving yellow lines, solid double white lines, solid lines next to dotted white lines, blind spots, flashing Yield signs, thick green arrows, speed limits, school crossings, and roundabouts is simply too challenging and too adult for me. The mere thought of gauging distances by looking into little mirrors *while* moving forward makes me want to implode into an agitated crumb of matter.

But I do have a driver's license.

Junior year of high school, I chose to take Driver's Ed with everyone else. After receiving a permit, I was thrust into oncoming New York City traffic with cursing taxi drivers and frightened pigeons. I've pretty much blocked the whole thing out, but do recall that the teacher smoked an entire pack of Camel Lights per lesson and often screamed, "Please Lord!" while spastically intervening with his side of the dual brakes and steering wheel. Eventually a group of us were shipped via yellow school bus to a barren testing facility in Long Island where there was a lot of chewed gum hanging off of signposts and cement ledges. My friends assumed they would pass—they had been driving every weekend since they were, like, three years old, to and from their country houses upstate. But every one of them failed. Each for some totally random small error, like going just a tad too slow when leaving the fake intersection.

When it was my turn, I got into a small red vehicle and noticed that my tester was excessively wrinkly. *Elderly.* While clearing phlegm from his throat, he slowly stated, "You. My dear. You are my first. Testee. Please take it away."

I felt like I'd been dropped into a surgical residency and told to operate. He started the car and we cautiously chugged forward. I was so consumed with gripping my hands at "ten" and "two" that I forgot to stop at the first Stop sign. He said, "You overlooked. Stopping at that sign, dear."

I tried to parallel park but hit the curb at a wide angle. He said, "You aren't allowed. To hit the curb. Like that, dear."

When we pulled up to the end of the course, it was clear to both of us that I was a potential menace to society and should be banned from all roads.

"So. Dear. Would you. Promise to practice?" he asked.

"Uh . . . yeah?"

"Alrighty, then. It's a pass. Congrats, dear."

I decided to get the license and renew it so I'd have a legit ID and never have to carry a bulky passport to bars. But NO WAY was I ever going to get behind the wheel again.

But then, many years later, I found myself living in West Hollywood and was told that L.A. cabs are too expensive, and that there is no real way to get around on buses and subways, and that I had to consider, at least for a split second, taking a proper driving lesson just to see if driving could ever be a part of my future.

I went online, and the schools in my area were listed alphabetically. First was the prestigious A Driving School. Perfect. On the phone I stressed my lack of knowledge, pleading for their most gifted instructor. The woman on the other end barked, "Ma'am, you need to have a permit to sign up for a lesson. You got a permit, right? You clearly know something if you have a permit." I told her, "No, you don't understand, I have a *license*. It means nothing. I know *nothing*. Please send the permit booklet and someone who knows what they're doing."

An hour later, Mikey arrived at my door. He couldn't have been older than eighteen, and had four or five gold chains around his neck. One of them said "WASSUP" in large metal cursive. He had a carefully shaped, prickly brown mustache. Since there was only one steering wheel in his student vehicle, I cautiously got into the dirty passenger seat for an initial demonstration. He drove me around ranting, "You go this way, another car comes around the corner and you don't look, it's BOOOOOM! You all dead. You want that? No. So you turn. Okay?"

When I asked why exactly one cannot make left turns at a red light he answered, "Wendy, don't be all philosophically about it. Just DON'T DO IT."

As he ran through Stop signs he groaned, "Wendy, do not develop my bad driving habits, okay? You would stop there. Okay?"

After we switched seats, and I was put in charge of steering, his cell phone kept blaring out a ring tone version of "Electric Avenue." He kept answering and yelling at his girlfriend, who had apparently taken too long to get ready the prior weekend for a big deal rocking house party. The phone calls were interrupted by screaming Dodgers fans on the radio. (He had to listen to the game—there was money riding on it.) Every few minutes, he'd bark, "C'mon, Wendy—speed up! If you drive like this all granny-like, you gonna get someone behind you yelling, 'FUCK YOU BITCH!' You want that? No. So you gotta go faster, okay?"

When we eventually made it back to my house, my knees were weak and my brain was in pain. Somehow I'd returned knowing less than when I started. I was left with a negative understanding of driving.

As a last resort, I decided to go ahead and risk a potential breakup and seek assistance from Amos. For two hazardous weeks, I drove him around in his black Honda Accord. I had a tendency to freeze, physically and emotionally, before making slight adjustments to the gas, brake, or steering wheel. Amos yelled, "NOW! GO NOW!" but for heaven's sake, I couldn't act that quickly. Um, I was accustomed to the good ol' trustworthy system of weighing pros and cons.

During this rather tumultuous period, Amos and I had five escalating fights regarding my slow reaction time at intersections and on busy streets. Three of these ended with me crying, "I just can't do it! Stop pushing me! Why am I so alone in this world?!" I watched pellets of sweat drip down his neck while he waved apologetically and mouthed, "I'm so sorry" or "Take another parking spot, this will take a while" to other drivers staring in disbelief.

I said, "Well, surely people assume I'm learning." But Amos explained that those who block intersections after forgetting to turn left in time are seen as "stupid," and those who cut others off after forgetting to get in the right lane are seen as "assholes."

I cannot express how upsetting it was to discover that I'd been incorrectly regarded as a douche bag. I pride myself on being a nice, decent, giving person. A good listener. A loyal friend. So I made a sign for the car out of poster board that read, "NEW

TO DRIVING." The black letters were outlined with bright yellow, lemon-scented Magic Marker. I planned to tape it to the back window so that if someone honked and cursed at me, I could look back at them and go, "Can't you read *signs*, asshole? I'm *New to Driving*."

Because Amos fancies himself a manly, advanced, coordinated kind of guy, he refused to let me attach the sign to his car. "I don't want it there when I'm driving," he whined. He said it was time for me to buy my own car anyway because I was probably going to mess his up with some sort of candy/gum accident at any moment.

Buying a car might be the only thing on the planet I understand less than using a car, so I massaged Amos's back as he researched used cars on the Net. He reported that, unlike other brands, 1996 or 1997 Honda Accords had been tested for both front and side impacts. I figured the more impact-testing the better, so we conducted a search on Craig's List and came up with ten to fifteen strangers in the Los Angeles area who claimed to have old Honda Accords in good condition.

First we met up with Terri in West L.A. The car looked like, I dunno, a *car*, something I would never operate properly or understand or appreciate. It was a bland off-white color, but that didn't even matter. I usually care about the color of things I buy, but a *car*—color seemed irrelevant because in a matter of weeks it would be totaled or dented and scratched. Plus, I refused to be someone who cared about what their car looks like.

Amos and I got in—me in the driver's seat, him sitting next to me—and Terri crawled in the back so I could do a test-drive around the block. Test-driving a car when you barely know how to drive is super scary, but test-driving a car when you barely know how to drive with the current owner of the car in the backseat is genuinely entertaining. The joy I got from looking in the rearview mirror and watching her expression go from wide-eyed/hopeful to crinkled eyebrows/alarmed made up for my paralyzing fear. Amos felt the need to apologize, "She just learned how to drive."

Terri turned a little pale but tried to stay positive. "Oh. How exciting." She gripped the side of the seat cushion.

After one lap, Amos asked, "Do you have time for us to go around the other corner again or—"

"No. You can pull in now."

I squeezed into the driveway knowing I couldn't buy the car anyway because the gray leather seats smelled too leathery. Leather was not going to allow me to inhale with ease, and I was certain I was going to have to do a lot of deep relaxation breathing on the road.

Next we met Tom and his Honda SE in a lot in Santa Monica. I was excited about Tom because his voice had sounded precise on the phone. He overemphasized consonants, and someone who has an anal way of talking probably has an anal way of living and an anal way of keeping their car in spiffy condition. When Tom finally approached us, he was everything I'd imagined and more—a tall, lanky man with a clenched jaw holding a huge folder of documents. We said a brief formal hello, and he encouraged us take it for a spin.

On the phone, Tom had described the car as being "champagne." Because I don't drink alcohol, I had confused champagne with red wine and expected it to be a cool burgundy color. But the car turned out to be a watered-down dark beige. Which was fine, whatever, I only cared about safety.

Amos performed the test-drive this time because I was too spent from my trip around the block with Terri. As we turned the second corner, we agreed that the car seemed brand new. It smelled like a recently vacuumed room at a Days Inn. We drove back to Tom, and Amos told him we'd buy it.

"Okay, well, I have about twenty people interested right now," he replied. "So . . . I'll be in touch."

"Oh, but we'll pay you now," Amos added. "A cashier's check."

"As I said, some others are interested and I have a few more appointments tomorrow so I'll let you know soon."

"What are you basing your decision on?"

"Highest bidder, I guess. But I'm not going to ask for more than the price I listed."

"So . . . wait, what? We will pay the listed price."

"Terrific. I'll let you know when I make my decision."

Even I saw the flaw in his car logic. All we could do was nod politely. As a last pathetic attempt I added, "We'll be proud parents!? We'll love and cherish it!?" But he seemed immune to my charm and we awkwardly said good-bye.

Two days later I decided not to buy a car after all because, who was I kidding, I'd never be one of those people who could drive around all by themselves. But as I looked up taxi services to see if they offered a special rate for incredibly frequent customers, I got a call on my cell phone.

"Hello, Wendy? It's Tom . . . from the car. I just want to let you know that . . . I have selected *you* for the car."

I paused. And slowly realized that I'd WON A CAR! I'd have to pay, yes, but I was CHOSEN!! CHOSEN!!

I pretended to be calm. "Oh, okay, great, thank you so much."

"So I have to go and call the other people and let them know, but barring any complications with that process, the car is yours."

"Great!" What complications? Someone becomes suicidal from the news, and he's got no choice but to ease their pain and give them the vehicle?

Tom called at 8 a.m. the next morning to arrange to meet at the DMV that afternoon, to do a change of title. Amos had already left for a job interview, so I took a ridiculously expensive cab ride and met Tom in the general information line. When he assured me he had taken the car to get a whole workup, I believed the crap out of him. This man was a stickler for the rules. I tried to make some sort of joke to ease the silence.

"So, like, is there something I should know about the car . . . vacations it's taken, places it's been, likes, dislikes . . . would you like me to send pictures to you of its growth?"

"No."

"So how did I make the cut?"

"In the end it was between you and this other girl. Ultimately you seemed more enthusiastic."

After the whole title issue was taken care of, Tom and I got in the car in the parking lot and he began showing me some of the nifty little hidden features. "If you press this button on the door, all the windows will be locked. So, say, if a young child were sitting in the back, he or she couldn't get carried away zooming the window up and down."

I nodded but thought, *That actually sounds fun. Shit, I wish I were the kid in the backseat and not the one having to drive this thing.*

As he continued to describe the added benefits of my new gadget, he must have noticed the extreme concentration and bewilderment plastered across my face because he became more and more thorough. "And here is the radio, ya know, the volume, the tracks, the air-conditioning, ya know, the fan . . . the windshield wipers . . . the turn signal . . . you do know how to signal, right? Here's the *ignition.* You . . . have . . . to put the key *in* and *turn* it—do you know how to drive?"

A second later, Tom's wife, an Amazon three times his size, in a blue business suit, came running toward us to take him home.

"I'm sorry I'm late! I'm here, Tom. Wendy, I must apologize for my husband. He's . . . well, he's very emotionally attached to the car."

All defensive, Tom sternly replied, "I take care of all my things and the car is one of my things!" He removed a piece of lint from the passenger seat. "I'm going to have to drive the girl back to her house, Linda. She's obviously not ready to drive it. Follow me there."

I was more than happy to let him drop me off.

When I got in my car the next day to drive to the nearby Rite Aid, I thought, *Is this minor errand really, really worth risking death? Both mine and others? Do I really need Swiffer mop refills? Maybe I can get down on my hands and knees and wash the kitchen floor with Oil of Olay astringent. Do I really need to get my birth control prescription? Maybe we'll get lucky with the rhythm method.*

Ultimately, I concluded I had to force myself out of my bubble. So I busted out my "NEW TO DRIVING" sign and Scotchtaped it to the back window in hopes that the words would alert others to the treacherous situation at hand. I needed a wide berth.

On the ride to the pharmacy, I actually fell head over heels for the car. It had nothing to do with how the car drove (I don't know what good brakes or good gas are supposed to feel like) but I could really hear the car saying, "Don't worry, Wendy, we'll get through this together." In a low, soothing, casual tone, not a futuristic electronic one, like in *Knight Rider*.

When I got to Rite Aid, I felt like the most accomplished person on earth. Not only did I arrive at my destination without causing a major accident, but I *parked*. Not in a parallel way, but I managed to plant myself in between two other cars without sticking out or blocking anything. For the most part. It reminded me of the contentment I felt after putting a jacket on by myself for the first time.

As I approached the store, the electric double doors flew open. For some reason, electronic sensors (the ones on doors, faucets, and ATMs) don't always automatically recognize my presence, so it felt as if some high-up Rite Aid honcho had been informed of my triumph. As I made my grand entrance, I imagined I was Will Smith's character in *Independence Day* as he struts out of the spaceship in slow motion after saving humanity. I walked through the aisles aimlessly, desperately wanting to yell out, "I made it, people!"

I waltzed to the back of store to pick up my birth control and felt compelled to blurt the news to the pharmacist. "There should be two prescriptions under my name . . . and, um, I dunno, it's just rather exciting, actually, because I just drove here and I just learned how to drive and it's really scary but I got here so . . . anyway, it's kinda exciting." The Indian woman looked back at me and replied, "That's so great. You totally did it. And you can do it again." Her supportive response sent confidence through my entire body.

But not enough to make it home from Rite Aid.

While I'd been rejoicing by the bulk candy section, two new cars had slid into the tight spaces on either side of mine. When I tried to extricate myself from the cluster, I somehow ended up *in* a pole. I was forced to call Amos who had to take a cab and free the car with minimum scratching.

On the way home we decided to officially name my car Mini Driver. I'm against naming cars because it's downright corny, but I had to make an exception to my own rule because traveling around with a pun based on an English actress whom I've always found somewhat annoying made me feel more at ease.

* * *

I've tried operating Mini Driver eleven times by myself since Rite Aid. One of these times was a trip to the local mall. When entering the parking garage through the narrow, yellow plank, it was clear that you were supposed to pick up an electronically dispersed parking ticket from a small machine on your left by rolling down the window and snatching the stub. But as I approached, my arm wouldn't reach. I wasn't close enough. And because there was a stream of thirty impatient cars behind me, I wasn't able to back up and redo it. So I took an extra ten minutes to slide three-fourths of my body out the window. I dangled dangerously from my thighs, successfully grabbing the needed slip. When I inched back into my seat and continued up the rest of the plank, I was sweating profusely but feeling good about myself. Yes, I was embarrassed that I hadn't driven close enough to the machine, but I have short arms and assumed everyone behind me would understand my plight. Plus, I had the sign in the back of my car. But as I went upward, a man pulled up next to me and yelled, "Why didn't you just open the door and get out of the fucking car?"

I honestly hadn't thought of that. I didn't know that was allowed. I pathetically muttered, "Because I'm . . . *new to driving*?"

On the way home I was driving along, trying my darnedest to FOCUS, when all of a sudden, I heard tons of loud piercing honking. All at once. I nearly broke down in tears trying to figure out how I'd fucked up. Was I leaking gas? Was my signal on? Was I going in the wrong direction? Somebody tell me, *please*. Then I realized I'd driven by an intersection with a group of protesters holding up signs that read, "Honk for Peace."

* * *

It's just so frustrating because every time I turn a corner in the car I feel like I'm in an entirely new land. I cannot keep track of rights and lefts or rotate grids in my head. It feels like I'm trying to carry numbers over in a hard math equation while experiencing a migraine. Even in Manhattan, if I'm walking uptown and quickly stop into a store, nine times out of ten I will leave and walk two or three blocks downtown until I realize some of the awnings look a little too familiar. I'm a native New Yorker who actually asks tourists for directions.

At least when I'm walking, though, I know I can approach five or six people for help until I find the right directional answer. I've tried seeking advice while driving by yelling through the window when other cars have pulled up beside me, but drivers either don't hear me or purposely ignore my cries. Or the light turns green and they rush off and abandon me. The car is a baffling bubble of solitude. I'm forced to carry on a surreal internal dialogue in which I seek advice *from myself.* Even though I've told myself a hundred times that I don't have the kind of information I'm looking for.

HOWEVER.

I will admit one thing.

There was one brief driving moment a few weeks ago—one moment—when I forgot about imminent death. I was on Melrose Avenue. It was mid-afternoon, the sun was glaring, palm trees were looming overhead, and I could hear the distant buzz of a helicopter. After taking pleasure in the faint clicking sound of the turn signal, I made the smoothest left ever onto a suburban side street. I smiled, leaned back, glanced at the rearview mirror, and moved my hands from "ten" and "two" to "eight" and "four." I felt like I was a responsible mom picking up a snotty-nosed little boy for a carpool. Like I could have picked out a down jacket in five minutes. Like I would have agreed to a nature hike. But I was still me. Only a grown-up version or something. It was kind of fun.

And then I took a door off of a Mercedes.

A guy opened his door just as I drove by and no one was hurt and the insurance company says it was technically his fault. But, holy shit.

And yet, I swear, right before it happened, I experienced a real adult moment.

Last week, my mother took off work and came to visit us for the first time on the West Coast. After driving her to the big suburban supermarket and cruising along the winding roads of the Hollywood hills, she was so inspired by my driving progress that she decided she'd get her learner's permit within the year. It would come in handy during her weekends in the country with Kevin. I even ended up giving her a driving lesson in an empty lot near my house.

If only my grandfather had been around to film it.

We were crouched, side by side, in my slightly banged up Honda Accord. There was a new sign in the back window: "RELATIVELY NEW TO DRIVING."

"Wendaay, the mirror won't adjust. I can't see behind me. And what's that sound? Which button is for the mirror?"

"I'm not sure. I've never figured out the side mirrors. Amos told me that it's easier to just use the top center one."

"That mirror looks foggy. Do you have someone clean these windows?"

"Just make sure your shoulder pads don't block your blind spot, Mom. Is the seat comfortable? You have to be able to reach both pedals."

"Should I not be wearing pumps for this?"

"Probably not. Just move forward like a tiny bit. A tiny bit. Tap the gas for a second. No one is around."

"Is that gum stuck to the radio?"

"Yes. Tap the gas."

"Tap?"

"Just for a moment."

And we were off.

acknowledgments

Infinite thanks to Laureen Rowland, who took a chance and believed in me from the very beginning, to Danielle Friedman for all her editorial brilliance, and to my magnificent agent and friend Lydia Wills, who thought of transforming my one-woman show into an actual book in the first place and whose encouragement and patience knows no bounds. Enormous thanks to the amazing Elizabeth Keenan, Jason Gobble, Patti Pirooz, Sabila Khan, Jason Yarn, Carl Weiner, Tucker Voorhees, Dave Becky, Jim Hess, Josh Lieberman, Nancy Rose, Ellis Levine, Kevin Thomsen, and everyone at Hudson Street Press and Penguin who helped in the publishing process. Natasha Glasser, you are a savior.

The following people were so helpful and calming during the writing process, I can barely handle it. I want to hug them until they burst: Kylie Fox, Hilary Liftin, Brangien Davis, Erin Keating, Adam Reid, Robbie Chaffitz, Susie Banikarim, Katie Broomfield, Rachel Ruane, Jessi Klein, Caroline Wells, Joe Schiappa, Lisa Kaplan, Fred Glasser, Regan Toews, Amanda Elliston, John Grey, Emily Gitter, Jody Lambert, Emily Voorhees, Todd Rosenberg, Mike Campbell, Garret Savage, Helen Bain, Zoe Langsten, Christie Smith, Samantha Abeysekera, Robin Epstein, Alex Raben, Angela Howard, John Newman, Stuart

Berkowitz, Todd Drucker, R. T. Arnold, Nick Kroll, Adam Cole-Kelly, Salil Gandhi, Lou, Allison, Charlie and Annie Wallach, Marg Elliston, Fred Harris, Jonathan Ruane, Mike Elliston, Roberta Gardner, Gail Eisenberg, Marshall, Adam and the entire Cordell family, Brendan Vaughn and his hipster baby, the entire Comedy Central gang, Leslie Patent, Laura Beech, Alisa Hall, Maya Kremen, Soomee Lubin, Kenan Minkoff, George Minkoff, Lauren Weedman, Judith Kampfner, Sheila Head, Allison Castillo, Dara Greenwood, Steve Weiss, Casey Kait, Naomi and Brian Steinberg, Dan Powell, Jen Goldstein, Alissa Shipp, Rachel Meeropol, Ivy Meeropol, and Joyce.

Thanks to the following people for their amazing advice and support: Jonathan Ames, Sarah Vowell, Amy Sohn, Lori Gottlieb, Anthony King, Seth Morris, the UCB Theater, Liesl Schillinger, Zoe Pagnamenta, Conan Smith, Wendie and Phil Adelman, Rob Battles, Show "N" Tell, Sit "N" Spin, Fresh Yarn, Lou Viola, Amanda Stern, and David Blauner.

Also, thanks to everyone who was mentioned in these stories and a big special shout-out to Hugh Grant and Carly Simon.

Amos, thanks for putting up with the madness.

Mom and Grandma, thanks for being such good sports.

And finally, thanks to you, the reader, for listening to my stories and completing my microthrills.

about the author

Wendy Spero is the author of the one-woman shows *Microthrills* and *Who's Your Daddy?*, which had a year-long run at the Upright Citizens Brigade Theater in Manhattan before being produced at the Edinburgh International Fringe Festival. She has been named "Best Female Comic of the Year" by *Time Out New York* and one of the "Top Ten Standout Stand-ups Worth Watching" by *Back Stage* magazine. She has performed on NPR, Comedy Central, VH1, and NBC, and has written for *Esquire*, the *New York Times*, and the comical anthology *Bar Mitzvah Disco* (Crown, 2005). She is currently cowriting a television pilot for HBO.

Wendy continues to perform regularly in both New York and Los Angeles, and she currently lives in West Hollywood with her boyfriend, Amos.